NEW TRA
TO THE TOWER
by
Steve Palmer

1st Edition - 1965 2nd Edition - 1997 3rd Edition - 2004 4th Edition - 2012 & 2016

@ STEVE PALMER - TRAMROAD HOUSE

Printed by Hesketh Press, Fleetwood.

PRELUDE by the AUTHOR, Steve Palmer

Undoubtedly 2012 is a historic date in the history of the Blackpool tramway, when at Easter the eleven mile inter-urban light-railway starts again, with a new generation of trams. The Flexity 2 articulated trams built by Bombardier – costing two million pounds each – have been funded, together with the new depot and updated system. This was a financial consolation by the previous Government, when Blackpool failed to get a National Casino. Undoubtedly this has provided Blackpool with a modern system, while it has survived since it was created by B & F Tramroad Company in 1898 and merged with the Promenade tramway in 1920. With the Centenary in 1985, Blackpool successfully proved that it was the only survivor of the British tramway scene, demonstrating this with a 20 tramcar procession! In 2010, the 125th Anniversary was celebrated, in contrast to the reconstruction of the system for the future.

I well recall my first production of a book in 1965, at a time when I felt it was necessary to record a larger tramway and its fleet. Once again in 2012, at a time of change and the survival of historic trams, it is important to present the new generation and recall the past! I hope you will find the book interesting, in many ways.

HOLD TIGHT!

STEVE PALMER

Steve Palmer standing next to 008, pointing at the L plate in 2012.   *R.P. Fergusson*

Acknowledgements

I acknowledge all the help given by:
Dave Hislop was Chief Engineer B.T.S.
The Gazette, Blackpool.
Glynn Wilton,
Former Curator of National Tramway Museum, Crich Tramway Village, Crich, Derbyshire. Photos from collection by **M.J.O'Connor & H.B. Priestley.**
Present photographers:
R.P. Fergusson, Terry Daniel, Ian McLoughlin, Bryan Grint, John Garnham, Peter Fitton & late John Fozard,
Tramway Map by **Terry Daniel.**

Contents

Pharos Lighthouse in Fleetwood with the new Flexity tram passing in 2012.

Author

General Managers

John Lancaster	1885 – 1910	25 years
Charles Furness	1910 – 1932	22 years
Walter Luff	1933 – 1954	22 years
J.C. Franklin	1954 – 1974	20 years
D.L. Hyde	1974 – 1986	12 years

Managing Directors

Tony Depledge	1986 – 2001	16 years
Steve Burd	2001 – 2009	8 years
Trevor Roberts	2009 – 2014	5 years
Jane Cole	2014 – present	

Side view of 001 driver's cab with the driver waiting for the traffic lights at Little Bispham. *Author*

On 18 November 2011,with 001 Flexity 2 on its first journey to Fleetwood, Here it has stopped at Stanley Road for inspection of the loading platform clearance. *Author*

Blackpool Tramways - At a Glance

Operator	-	Blackpool Transport Services Limited
Managing Director	-	Jane Cole
Tram Fleet	-	26 passenger trams, 12 Heritage, 3 Illuminated trams, 1 Works.
Mileage	-	11.5 route miles (6.5 street route miles finished 1961-3)
Gauge	-	4 foot 8.5 inches
Line Voltage	-	600 volts DC

Dates to Remember

29 Sept 1885	-	Official opening of the Conduit Tramway System
7 August 1897	-	Conduit track laid along Lytham Road and Station Road
11 July 1898	-	Blackpool & Fleetwood Tramroad Company, tram 4 runs first
13 June 1899	-	Overhead line system adopted in Blackpool Borough
30 May 1901	-	Trial run on the new Marton route round Blackpool
13 June 1902	-	Talbot Square & Layton Cemetery new route opened
1 January 1920	-	Blackpool bought Blackpool & Fleetwood Tramroad Company
2 October 1926	-	Tramway extended along New South Promenade
1 April 1933	-	Walter Luff's Five Year Plan for modernisation began
19 October 1936	-	Conversion of Layton & Central Drive to buses
December 1946	-	First resilient-wheel modernised car 303 on Marton route
5 June 1952	-	First post-war car – Coronation 304 – was delivered
9 April 1958	-	Inaugural run of trailer-car set 276-275 went to Fleetwood
Easter 1958	-	Double-deck trams ran to Fleetwood for the first time
16 June 1960	-	New MCW trailer T1 delivered to Rigby Road Depot
29 Sept 1960	-	Processions to celebrate 75th Anniversary of the tramway
29 October 1963	-	Closure of Squires Gate route and Marton South Pier line
28 October 1962	-	Closure of Marton route and Marton depot
27 October 1963	-	Closure of North Station via Dickson Road & Bispham Depot
29 Sept 1985	-	Centenary of Promenade Tramway with 20 tram procession
1 July 1898	-	Centenary of Fleetwood route commemorated by B & F 2 & 40
12 July 1998	-	B & F Centenary Day – procession of 14 trams to Fleetwood
23 October 2000	-	Return of Standard 147 to Blackpool from U.S.A.
29 Sept 2010	-	125th Anniversary procession for Promenade Tramway
Easter 2012	-	Inauguration of the new light-rail line with 16 Flexity 2 cars

An interesting scene of track laying at the new Starr Gate depot in October 2010, showing the track fan and the service terminus on the left. (opposite) In February 2011 with Engineering Car 754 using its diesel engine for rigging the new overhead in front of the depot. *Author*

Electrical Details

The system is supplied from the National Grid and rectified to 600 volts d.c., originally by five mercury arc rectifiers situated at Bond Street S.S., Gynn Square, Bispham Depot, Thornton Gate and Copse Road Depot, Fleetwood. The electrical department of Blackpool Transport looked after the overhead line, running-repairs and rewiring. The overhead hangs at nineteen feet above street level, and most cars collect current through pantographs, while others have trolley poles with fixed heads and 6 inch wheels. Section feeders and breakers are indicated by orange-diamonds on the poles with them. In 1995-6 the system was rewired and restructured with new poles with stainless steel bracket-arms, from Starr Gate to Thornton Gate. New sub-stations were constructed at Pleasure Beach loop, Manchester Square, Metropole, Gynn Square, and Little Bispham, and existing sub-stations at Bispham and Thornton Gate were refurbished. Overhead north of Thornton Gate was renewed in 2003, with new substations at Broadwater, Copse Road and finally a new substation was built at Bold Street terminus in 2012. Both depots – at Rigby Road and Starr Gate – have their own sub-stations.

Tram Stops, Speeds & Signs

Originally REQUEST & COMPULSORY STOPS were shown by circular polo-shaped signs, painted green and cream. The EEC stop sign has been used with the shape of a tram and Tram Stop + Place-name, and at each stop the timetable is shown. With the modernisation of the tramway in 2012, stops have been reduced from 65 to 37 and raised platforms provided with seats and shelters at many, a location name-sign is clearly shown, together with lighting. FACING POINTS: Have always been shown by black dividing lines on white boards surmounted by a red triangle, signs now indicate power-points SPEED LIMITS: At curves and road crossings, poles are fitted with white diamonds showing speeds in black numbers, for example Gynn Square and Cleveleys curves are 12 mph. Also shown: stops at 4 mph, Promenade track at 16 mph, and reservation north of Cabin at 30 mph. On the new system, road crossings are controlled by signals for trams, indicating horizontal bars for stop and vertical bar for proceeding. These are co-ordinated with the traffic lights introduced, starting with Little Bispham road-crossing, and continuing north of there with ten road-crossings to Fleetwood.

Track – Permanent Way

The standard gauge of 4ft. 8.5 ins is used for the system, with B.S. Section 8 grooved rail used for street track and along the Promenade, road crossings and Starr Gate, Pleasure Beach & Little Bispham loops. Tramway reservation uses 95lb flat-bottom rail, held by spring-clips to concrete sleepers, with rubber insert pads. On reservation curves, double bullhead-rail is used, held in double-chairs upon wooden sleepers. By 2012 all reservation track has been relaid, improving the quality of ride. Also, a new two-way junction has been laid at North Pier, providing a future route to North Station. Former street-track at Metropole is now on reservation, and Fleetwood terminus-track has been doubled into Pharos Street.

Trams First Began In 1885

Tuesday, 29th September 1885 proved to be a fete day for Blackpool, with the official opening of the new tramway as part of the Lifeboat Fete. Civic dignitaries from all parts of Lancashire gathered to witness a double-event. The town was in a holiday mood: large streamers floated from the lamp standards and shop keepers had decorated their shop frontages. The inauguration of the first electric street tramway was said to "posses elements of unique interest", and "gives Blackpool its own place as a pioneer". The local newspaper, while admitted that electric traction had already been tried elsewhere, dismissed them as "early trials" in a contemptuous vein.

"Other towns have the lead in adopting electricity as a motive power for tramway use, but in the case of Brighton, the Volks Electric Tramway is little more than a toy, and the line running in the North of Ireland is of a type quite different."

So much for Volks and the Giant's Causeway Tramway, but an element of truth existed despite this bombastic statement. Undoubtedly Michael Holroyd Smith's system introduced the electric tramway to the streets of Britain, and made urban mass transportation possible for the first time. It remains to the eternal credit of Blackpool that the invention was looked upon not with suspicion but as "one of the fairy tales of science". So to the great day and an eye-witness account:

Recreating a century-old scene in 1985, with conduit-car 4 and passengers appropriately dressed.
Ian McLoughlin

A crowded scene on 29th September 1985 at North Pier, with conduit-car 4 and Dreadnought 59 waiting for the civic party, ready for leading the procession of twenty trams to Pleasure Beach. Author

"Handsome in design and elegant in every detail of its construction, the car was brought up immediately opposite the lifeboat launching ground. Here 5 came and there it went palpably without assistance, showing the magic of adapted human knowledge. The crowd in the neighbourhood of the car and on the pier was simply astounding. Mr. Holroyd Smith had the honour to demonstrate the utility of electricity as a motive-power for tramway propulsion – an invention which may yet revolutionise the vehicular traffic of the world."

Prophetic words indeed, and Michael Holroyd Smith was conscious of the significance of his invention, when he presented Alderman Harwood – the Mayor of Manchester and opener of the line – with an ebony and brass handle, upon which was inscribed: "Presented to Alderman Harwood, Mayor of Manchester, by Mr. Holroyd Smith engineer, on the occasion of his Worship inaugurating the Blackpool Electric Tramway, September 29th 1885." The handle was made by Smith, Baker and Company of Manchester, the firm which had made the controllers for the ten cars. Thus the new tramway – and the lifeboat SAMUEL FLETCHER - were well and truly launched, and Blackpool was again a pioneer!

A century later, on 29th September 1985, the original ebony and brass handle was produced by the Harwood family, and used to drive conduit-car 4 at the head of a Centenary procession of twenty cars.

In September 1886, Holroyd Smith read a paper before the British Association at Birmingham, in which he described his Blackpool Tramway system. Some of the early difficulties emerge from his talk, and the discussion which followed,and some interesting figures for operation were given. The number of passengers carried during a six-day week in the winter of 1885 was 2,393 at a cost of fuel and wages of under £24. In contrast, during the week ending September 4th 1886, which was at the height of the season, the number of passengers carried was 44,306, while the cost of wages and fuel was £45. The figures show that while the number of passengers increased twenty-two times the winter figure, the costs less then doubled, and demonstrated the unique value of the tramway for the first time. However, the promenade line had many disadvantages, which are here described by its inventor:

"The Blackpool line is nearly two miles in length. It is a single track, with ten passing loops and one length of double-line along central promenade. The engine house and car sheds are placed near the centre, and this position was selected as being the most convenient, and so offering considerable advantages from an electrical point of view. The roadway runs along the sea-coast facing directly west, and exposed to the full force of the wind and tide from the Irish Sea. So strong are the periodic storms that, though the road level is well above the ordinary high-water mark, the waves wash over in such volume that the road is flooded and the doors and windows of houses are occasionally beaten in. The difficulties in supplying electricity underground through the conduit in such a situation, are therefore unusually great. When the tide is over the line, the current of course makes earth. At one time it was intended to employ accumulators for haulage during flooding, and horses were occasionally used, but owing to the amount of shingle brought over, the grooves in the rails were filled, and the cars kept derailing. Trams working during the floodings has therefore been abandoned,"

A fascinating original view of two trams passing at North Pier in about 1900. Both trams are built by Lancaster Carriage Works, and each could be either smaller 3 or 4 and larger 5 or 6.

Author's Collection

A striking scene of 4 and 59 leading the procession, with Municipal guests in costume, on 29th September 1985. *John Garnham*

The generators, situated behind the depot in Blundell Street, could produce maximum force of 300 volts, but trouble was experienced with conductivity – the actual resistance being more than calculated. Holroyd Smith gave some interesting figures which show the fall in voltage over the line:

"At the tram shed, where the current was led direct to the conduit contactors, there was an electromotive force, and at Foxhall – the junction with the main line -210 volts. At the north end of the line –Cocker Street – it was reduced to 185 volts, and at the south end of the line – Victoria Pier – 168 volts."

He attributed this fall in voltage to poor joints and faulty connections, and pointed out that after a night of heavy rain or sea flood, there was a serious loss of conductivity. The efficiency of the generator was 90%, whereas that of the cars was only 45%, and thus more perfect insulation needed to be achieved.

In 1892 the Corporation took over from the Electric Tramway Company, switched the supply to its own power station, and extended the conduit line along Station Road in 1897, linking Lytham Road track with the Promenade track at Victoria Pier (South Pier). However after continuing problems of the tram system, and the successful example of the new Blackpool & Fleetwood Tramroad in 1898, in 1899 the overhead line was erected and the Board of Trade inspected it on 13th June. When it came into use on 21st June, the conduit was still live and could be used by cars having problems in losing their trolleys, until all was satisfactory. This was caused by the 20 foot trolley-poles, working at right-angles to the overhead mounted on short bracket-arms. While the conduit system was an interesting creation, Blackpool seashore tramway was unsuitable while London trams successfully operated on a large conduit system, until its closure in 1952.

The New Tramroad In 1898

The construction of the Blackpool & Fleetwood Tramroad commenced in 1897 by the Company, which could see the importance of linking the popular resort of Blackpool with the important seaport of Fleetwood. The construction of the line crossed the "bleak and rugged cliffs of Bispham and the desolate stretch of Norbreck", intending that it would open-up the coast for the visitors at Blackpool. This was a light-railway, with fixed stopping-places over the 8.5 miles, with street tramways at each end. Blackpool refused to allow the Company to construct its line along the sea-front to North Pier, having acquired Claremont Park in 1896, and thus the line was diverted along the back road to Talbot Road Station. From King Edward Avenue on the cliffs to the Station, the Borough built the line and leased it to the Company for 21 years, until 1919. In Fleetwood the Company constructed the line, with the option of the U.D.C. being able to buy it after thirty years. "The Experimental Opening – An Exhilarating Ride" came in 1st July 1898, when crossbench car 4 took a party of Tramroad Company Board, Blackpool Borough Council, Transport Department officials and the press for the first ride to Fleetwood. "A large number of people crowded the street in front of the Talbot Road Station, and gave a hearty send-off to the party at 3.10 p.m.". As "Father of Blackpool" Ald. Cocker said: "You cannot have smooth sailing on the first trial", since the street track was full of grit. Once outside the town boundary, the ride improved over the sleeper-track, and a passenger said: "The feeling was grand". When the tram arrived at Fleetwood Ash Street, a large crowd had gathered, and children from local Chaucer Road school cheered to welcome it. Car 4 was parked in Lord Street, while the party went for lunch at Mount Hotel, and the return journey stopped at Cleveleys Hotel, where Ald. Cocker proposed a toast for the Company's success.

Capturing the original scene with a Tramroad Company car on the cliffs, in a painting by the famous railway painter.
Eric Ramsbottom

1898 Crossbench car 2 passing Central Pier on 16 July 1998, during its visit for the Centenary
Author

The Board of Trade inspection took place on 13th July, and there were protests by bus owners that Warbreck Road was too narrow, and thus trams first operated from Gynn Square on the next day, until the road was widened by 29th September. The inspectors visited Bispham Depot and the generating power-station there, first travelling down the cutting from Bispham Top. A tram depot and yard was also built in Copse Road at Fleetwood, where there was a link with the railway line, thus able to bring coal to Bispham power-station. Also there was a small depot at Bold Street terminus, for the first and last cars each day. From 14th July the line opened, and for the first twelve months almost 1,500,000 passengers were carried over the system! Undoubtedly the commercial development of the Tramroad was seen in publicity: "One of the Joys of Life" and "Your Invigorating Ride to Blackpool". Of course the link with the daily sailing to the Isle of Man boat from Fleetwood also attracted riders on the trams. At the beginning, connection with the Company cars at Gynn Square was provided by landaus from the town centre. In 1900 Blackpool Borough built their own line to Gynn Squarer, through the recently acquired Claremont Park. While Blackpool used open-top cars – like the unique Dreadnoughts – the Tramroad Company operated single-deck crossbench cars with open sides and saloon cars – each suitable for the weather. The Manager John Cameron rode round the system once a day, ensuring efficient operation by 80 staff. He lived in a large house, called "Pooldhooie" near to Bispham depot, which today is the Conservative Club!

Circular Tour 1911 – 1960

Undoubtedly the introduction of the Circular Tour in 1911 was a memorable occasion. The new Manager Charles Furness ordered twenty-four Toastrack cars from United Electric Car Company at Preston, and were numbered 69 – 92. This innovation was a reaction to the increasingly popular excursions in chars-a-bancs. Charles Furness saw that the open electric trams would be ideal to attract visitors to Blackpool, in order to have a tour of the resort. The title CIRCULAR would follow the tramway system, starting in Talbot Square, crossing to the Promenade until South Pier where the Toastracks turned into Station Road, Lytham Road and at Royal Oak joined the Marton route. At Oxford Square the tour stopped, while a photographer captured the passengers on the Toastrack, and photographs could be bought that evening in Talbot Square. This was stopped in 1927, owing to traffic. Following tree-lined Whitegate Drive, it made the tour quite picturesque, until at Devonshire Square it turned towards the town centre passing Hippodrome, Winter Gardens and Opera House and ended opposite the North Pier. The fare was 6d, until it increased to 9d in 1932, when the tour was extended along New South Promenade, and Squires Gate Lane, passing the Airport before turning into Lytham Road. In 1927 six more Toastracks 161-166 were added, in order to cater for the long Circular Tour queues. In 1934 a new generation of Boat cars 225 - 236 replaced the older Toastracks. The Circular did not take place during WW11 and resumed in 1957 until 1961, when the Squire Gate route was replaced by buses. Subsequently in 1962 a new Promenade Circular was introduced, between Little Bispham & Pleasure Beach, but it was not the same novelty. Today it is still possible to ride on Toastrack 166 at N.T.M. Crich in Derbyshire!

Toastrack 79 seen on Circular Tour in Whitegate Drive, Marton. Since it is flying the Union Jack and French flag, this could be the time of First World War. *Author's Collection*

Toastrack 166 at the National Tramway Museum, filled with passengers on a sunny day.   *Author*

The Illuminations Started in 1912

It is now a hundred years since the Illuminations were inaugurated by the opening of the new Princess Parade in front of the Metropole Hotel by Princess Louise, and the first illuminated tram was De-Luxe 68 described as "the cynosure of all eyes". It was decorated by 3,000 bulbs and the effect was stunning when it toured the suburbs of Blackpool and Lytham St.Annes. In the following year, for the royal visit of 1913, 68 it was decorated by "LONG LIVE OUR KING & QUEEN". Following this, 68 permanently showed "WELCOME TO OUR VISITORS" on each side and "PROGRESS" at each end. Unfortunately the Illuminations ceased with the 1st World War, and did not resume until 1925 when they were revived by popular demand, following the chaos of the Carnival in 1924.

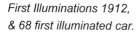

First Illuminations 1912,
& 68 first illuminated car.

The Gondola seen in the depot in the Fifties, showing its picturesque profile, with a Coronation car next to it.   *Author's Collection*

In addition to resuming decorated 68, it was decided that it would be a novelty to create a new illuminated tram from the frame and 4-wheel truck of Marton Box-car 28 in the Works. The elegant Gondola was created, with high curved-prows at each end, graceful pagoda-style roof in the centre and the hull was decorated by gold scrollwork. Undoubtedly the nautical effect was enhanced by painted canvas covering the 4-wheel truck and wavy rows of bulbs simulating water. Twenty passengers could board by climbing a ladder over the side and sit on the rattan-cane seats. In the first season the driver and conductor were dressed as Venetian gondoliers, much to the amusement of their colleagues on passing trams. Its seats were occasionally occupied by guests and a small orchestra was playing "The Gondoliers". Since the Gondola became a mobile part of the Illuminations, it helped to create the huge success of the event. In 1926, when it was the Golden Jubilee of Blackpool Borough, another illuminated tram, lifeboat "JUBILEE" was created from Marton Box-car 40. It showed the nautical effect by having illuminated sails which could be turned-round, and white lights hanging from the sides simulating safety-ropes. Unfortunately the Illuminations was terminated prematurely because of the National Miners' Strike, thus threatening power stations. On October 2nd they were switched on for the opening of New South Promenade and Stanley Park by Lord Derby. The three illuminated cars were seen each year until 1939, and resumed in 1949 with a new "PROGRESS" car replacing 68 and playing music as it toured. The Gondola and Lifeboat lasted until early Sixties.(See illuminated cars page 62-63)

The Two Tramways Merged in 1920

Since the Blackpool & Fleetwood Tramroad had been successful, commercial development took place along the coastal line. However the future of the Company was questioned when Bispham UDC became part of Blackpool in 1917, and the lease on its track in the Borough would end in 1919. Therefore negotiations secretly took place between the Mayor Ald. Lindsey Parkinson and Company Manager John Cameron. When Lancashire & Yorkshire Railway also became interested in purchasing the Tramroad Company. Blackpool Borough increased its offer to £284,000. This succeeded in securing its possession of the Tramroad on 1st January 1920. The amalgamation thus ensured the link between the Promenade tramway and the coastal line to Fleetwood. This enlarged Blackpool's fleet from 84 to 125 trams, and the Company trams were renumbered 101-141. The first task was to physically join the tracks with curves to the Promenade track at Gynn Square and to the Talbot Road line on the Layton route. While the ex-Company cars continued to operate the traditional route to Fleetwood, open-top Promenade trams would start operating to Bispham, once North Promenade track was moved on to reservation and Gynn Square new layout took place in 1924. Incidentally the old Gynn Inn was demolished to create the facility. Blackpool Transport modernised the Fleetwood line by re-aligning the Rossall track away from the front of Rossall School, to facilitate the construction of Broadway. In May 1925 a loop-line was built to the new Fleetwood Ferry terminus, with the trams now passing Pharos Lighthouse. Also the centre-poles for overhead in Lord Street were removed, and replaced by span-wires suspended from side-poles. A special tram now operated each day from North Pier at 9-45 to connect with the Isle of Man steamer from Fleetwood. Also the Goods & Mineral Service operated along the tramway, from the railway behind Copse Road depot to new Thornton Gate sidings, so linking Thornton Station with Cleveleys. Thus began a new future for the enlarged Municipal Tramway system.

Seen in Red Bank Road outside Bispham depot, two original B & F "Yanks" 122 & 121, joined together on trial, and the first has been rebuilt as a "Glasshouse".   *Author's Collection*

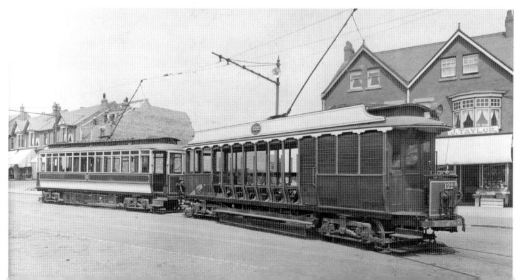

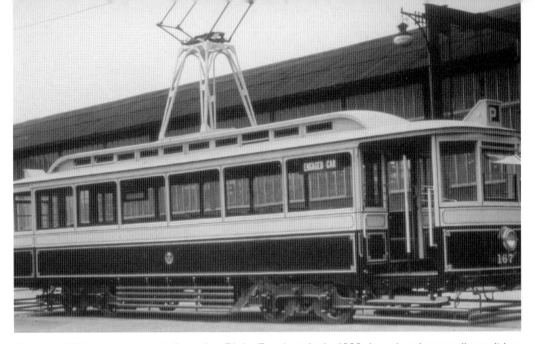

"Pullman" 167, having been delivered to Rigby Road works in 1928. In red and cream livery, it has a tall tower and a mounted pantograph, together with open platform.   *Author's Collection*

The Twenties in Blackpool was a momentous time for the Tramway, and especially the revival of the Illuminations in 1925. The opening of new workshops at Rigby Road was created by using four old aircraft hangars from Squires Gate airport, thus enabling the Transport Department to maintain the fleet. The first job was to rebuild ex-Company "Yank" cars as saloons named "Glasshouses". Importantly, they also built 35 new Standard cars and 6 Toastracks 161-166 between 1924 and 1927. Apart from these achievements, it should be added that two new Illuminated cars were built, the elegant "Gondola" built from Marton Box-car 28 in 1925 and the Lifeboat "Jubilee" from 40 in 1926. These became a trio, with De-Luxe 68, which was first created in 1912 when Illuminations started. The other new trams included seven Standards 146-152 built by Hurst Nelson of Motherwell, and ten new "Pullman" cars 167-176 built by E.E. Dick Kerr in 1928. These handsome saloon cars were fitted with pantographs, and were destined to operate a 12-minute service on the North Station & Fleetwood route, which lasted until 1961! Of course they became known as "Pantographs" and operated from Bispham depot, apart from 1935-1940, when they were at Rigby Road depot. A steeple-cab locomotive was acquired from English Electric in 1928, for towing the railway wagons conveying coal to Thornton Gate sidings. It is interesting that the final Standard tram 177 was built in 1929, from all the remaining suitable timber and fittings in the Works. During this decade there was a full programme of track-laying, including street-track to North Station, and making reserved-track tramway along North Promenade, by the creation of cantilever footpath over the Middle Walk. New South Promenade, with a tramway extension to Starr Gate was completed in October 1926. This made the future Fleetwood service eleven and a half miles long! In 1932, Manager Charles Furness finally reported to the Council that the volume of tramway traffic during the long evenings reached the achievement of 80 cars per hour! Then he continued being Electrical Engineer till 1936.

1933 – 1938 A New Generation of Trams

The appointment of new General Manager Walter Luff undoubtedly brought changes to Blackpool Transport, beginning with the introduction of a new streamlined railcoach, built by English Electric of Preston. Unlike previous trams they had produced, this was a single-decker with centre-entrance and comfortable seating in each saloon, with pointed fronts and twin indicators. The Transport Committee were so impressed by the design of the new tram, they allowed Walter Luff to order one. Number 200 arrived on 19th June in the new green and cream livery, it and went on display at Gynn Square siding for the interest of the Municipal Transport Managers Conference. It gave a demonstration run for the delegates from St. Annes Square to Fleetwood, and while they praised its smooth running on the reservation, some warned that there was a limited future for trams in Britain. However, in Blackpool an order for twenty-four more railcoaches was given, and these were to be used on the Blackpool & Fleetwood service. These would provide passengers with a comfortable journey, in competition with the rival motor coaches.

The railcoaches were a sensation when they first appeared on the Promenade, and the passengers waved passed old trams in order to ride on the new ones. It is said that upon entrance to the centre platform, they would remove their hats and look for the door-mats to wipe their feet! The saloons featured the moquette seats, half-drop windows, clocks at each end and the long sliding roof panels which could be opened. The conductor used a handle to wind them back on a sunny day, thus they became known as a "sunshine roof".

Also they were a big improvement for the drivers, who were now provided with enclosed cabs and seats, unlike hours standing in the wind and rain on the open-fronted trams.

The new streamlined railcoach 200, seen from the Dreadnought at the Tower in 1933. Notice the track turning towards Central Station.

Author's Collection

In August 1933 Walter Luff told the Transport Committee that a number of trams – like Dreadnoughts & Toastracks – were unsuitable for summer traffic, and showed them drawings of a new 94-seat open-topper and a modern 56-seat open single-decker. Mr. Luff reported that English Electric would build one of each type by the end of the year, and quoted a price for an additional twenty-five of each kind for the beginning of the 1934 Season. The Committee accepted the offer for the two demonstration trams, and waited until they had seen them. In January 1934 the Manager was able to report to his Committee that the two experimental cars would be soon ready for inspection. On 6th February they were delivered and appeared on the street siding at North Pier, and made an impressive pair: a large open-top double-decker and boat-like single-decker with canopy over its centre platform. The local press quoted: "There was a rush to see the new Blackpool trams in Talbot Square today, and people wholeheartedly expressed their praise." Consequently the propaganda succeeded in encouraging the Transport Committee to place a new order with E.E. Company, for 11 more open "Boats" and 12 more open-toppers. In addition they ordered 14 fully-enclosed double-deckers with luxury railcoach features. This began Walter Luff's "Five Year Plan" which would modernise the operation of trams in Blackpool!

The second year of the "Five Year Plan" was 1934, when it saw the delivery of the twelve open-toppers, which were numbered 237-249 including 226. They were unique in British tramway history because they were the only second generation of open-toppers. Although primarily designed for summer use, the design allowed the upper-deck to be closed off, by pulling down steel shutter-blinds on each of the two staircases. On the top deck were wooden reversible seats, the passengers being protected by the sides surmounted by stainless-steel hand rails. 54 passengers could be seated on the top deck, while the lower saloons could seat 40. With a total of 94 seats, the new cars surpassed the capacity of the Dreadnoughts which they intended to replace. The new double-deckers weighed 22 tons, thus having bogies with longer wheelbase, and Z6 controllers with field-shunt position, allowing them to run at 35 mph on the reservation.

The lower saloons were similar to the railcoaches, with reversible seating, half-drop windows and a grab-rail on the ceiling. The profile of the new open-toppers was more sloped than the upright appearance of 237.

Boat 225 seen outside the depot in Blundell Street, in 1934.
Author's Collection

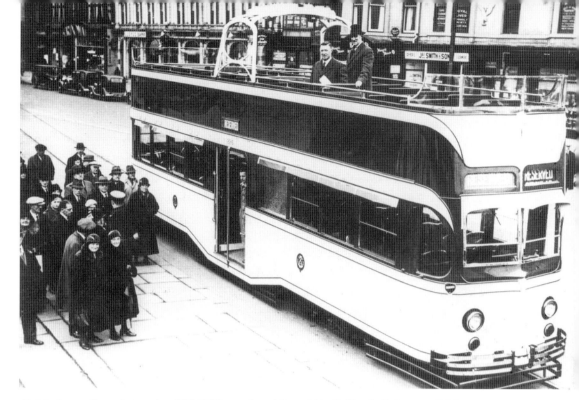

Public inspection of open-top 226 (237), on the siding at North Pier in February 1934.

Author's Collection

The open "Boat" car 225 was intended to give better features of the Toastracks, while incorporating the safety of the lower centre platform, side panels and a centre aisle. The other eleven "Boat" cars 226-236 were delivered during 1934 and had sides level with the seat-tops, thus higher than 225. Because 225 looked smaller, the staff called it "Little Willy". At first the "Boats" operated alongside their predecessors, the original 24 Toastracks were withdrawn by 1939. By the Easter of 1934, twenty-five of the vintage B & F type "Glasshouses" & "Box-cars" were replaced by the 24 railcoaches. These first went into service between North Station & Cleveleys, followed by the Fleetwood service. The production railcoaches were different from 200, being 3 feet longer with more room for the driver's seat. In the cab of 200 it had been difficult for the driver to sit down, because the cab was so narrow and thus was not comfortable. These railcoaches became popular having replaced older trams, which had higher steps and draughts inside.

By 15 December 1934, the first of the enclosed double-deckers 250-263 went into service on the Squires Gate route, replacing the traditional Standards, then only ten years old. Subsequently it was found that the "Balloons" – which they became named – remained on this service until 1961, when it closed. At the end of the 1934 season, twenty Dreadnoughts were taken to Copse Road depot where they were scrapped. After pressure in the press, Walter Luff phoned Fleetwood and told the workers to save the final one. The retention of 59 was announced, and the Evening Gazette responded: "Sometime in the future it may be possible to resurrect the old car and parade it on the Promenade". Well it did happen, in 1960 for the 75th Anniversary of the Tramway, and again in 1985 for the Centenary of the Tramway!

By 1935 there was a fleet of 64 streamlined cars, and Walter Luff decided on a new depot at Rigby Road to replace the old Blundell Street depot. The Borough Surveyor had prepared the plans by February, and tenders were accepted for pile-driving, steel-work, bricks and the track layout. The latter was being undertaken by Edgar Allen Company of Sheffield. Once construction had begun, it was proposed that the bus garage should be extended to align with the depot. This was designed to cater for the growing bus fleet, which included buses with centre-entrances and open single-deckers, following the current tramcar design. The new depot opened on 7 June 1935, taking over operation of the Fleetwood route from Bispham depot, which was reduced from a running-depot to a store for the remaining toastracks and Tramroad cars. With increased size, the new depot could take 108 cars on 18 tracks. Therefore in 1936 a further twenty of the E.E. railcoaches 264-283 were delivered before the season, and they replaced the remaining Box-cars with their corner-entrances and high steps which could delay rapid loading at frequent stops.

Lytham St. Annes blue-cars were still operating into Blackpool as far as Gynn Square, but they looked very old-fashioned compared with the new streamliners. Walter Luff was keen to take-over the track as far as St. Annes Square and therefore extend the reservation from South Promenade. Negotiations had been proceeding, but Lytham St. Annes did not want such operation in its Borough, and therefore the casting vote of their Mayor against the scheme, prevented St. Annes & Fleetwood tram service for ever. However at the end of the season, Blackpool trams operated finally on the street routes to Layton and Central Station via Central Drive. This was part of the "Five Year Plan" since the single-track caused traffic congestion in the town centre. The trams were replaced by new bus routes 22 and 23 operating from Layton to Marton Depot via Talbot Road, Promenade, Central Drive and Waterloo Road. All trams on the Marton route then operated to Royal Oak, and South Pier in the summer season.

Dreadnought 59 at Copse Road depot in 1940, having been saved from scrapping.

M. J. O'Connor NTM

At Bispham in April 1939, Pantograph car passes a Balloon. Notice the curve to the depot.

H. B. Priestley NTM

Modernising The Pantograph Cars & Ordering 20 More Trams!

Since the Pantograph cars were first introduced in 1928 for the Fleetwood line, it was necessary to retain and modernise them in 1936-7. They appeared in an entirely cream livery with only the roof in green, and the fleet numbers in numerals hard to see above the centre side pillar. The original tower was shortened by 15 inches from its tall height designed for pantographs and since replaced by trolleys. Platform folding-doors were fitted and new chrome windscreen-frames with air-operated wipers were an improvement. The front appearance was changed with a curved moulding round the indicator box. In the saloon all woodwork was grained and varnished, and the ceiling panels were painted in white enamel. Thus they all appeared by 1937, looked smarter than previously and were still on the North Station & Fleetwood route in the summer season. However it was surprising that in September 1936 Walter Luff was authorised to advertise for tenders to supply a further twenty single-deck cars. For the first time since the "Five Year Plan" began, the contracts were awarded to the Brush Company of Loughborough to make the bodies, E.M.B. to supply the bogies, and Crompton Parkinson & Allen West for the motors and controllers. This would bring the total streamlined fleet to over a hundred!

Pantograph 170 seen at Bispham in 1940, notice the hoods on the headlights and the Air Raid shelter next to it.
M. J. O'Connor NTM

1937 – "Journey's End for the Blue Cars"

Since the Lytham St. Annes Tramway was due to close on 27 April, it was proposed for Blackpool to acquire the track in Squires Gate Lane, and thus facilitate the continuation of the Circular Tours. On 28 April there was a special run for 41 from St. Annes Square to the depot in Squires Gate Lane for members of the Council. This last car, built in 1924 by English Electric, was an unvestibuled double-deck car with an open balcony, and mounted on a four-wheel P22 truck. It was retained at the depot afterwards, but unfortunately it was broken-up during the war, its metal given to the scrap-iron campaign. Following the closure of this tramway, Blackpool operated joint bus routes 11 &11A to Lytham St. Annes from Central Station.

Since this was the fourth year of the Plan, a new three-story Transport Office in art-deco style was built in Rigby Road, and can be seen to this day. Extension to the Works was made at this time, which included the body, painting and fitting shops. In August the double-track loop was opened at the Pleasure Beach, which facilitated the turning of many trams here. Walter Luff proposed building further loops at Little Bispham and Starr Gate, so construction started and they were both opened in 1938. Also plans were in hand for the complete relaying of the Lytham Road track and the Station Road branch line, at a cost of £45,075.

(above) 284 seen at Brush Works in Loughborough, showing its profile along with its trial front flare and the raised tower on an arch to allow the sliding-roof go underneath. NTM Collection

(opposite) Lytham St. Annes trams 47 and 8 passing near North Pier in 1932. Author's Collection

New Brush Railcars Arrived In 1937 &
A New Illuminated Car

The twenty new Brush cars 284-303 were delivered during the summer months. Although they had the same layout as the 45 E.E. railcoaches, they were quite distinctive and called railcars. The fronts were more tapered and as an innovation were the air-operated sliding platform-doors, which could be operated by the conductor or the driver. All the saloon windows could be fully wound-down, while the sunshine sliding roofs had much longer panels, moving under the trolley gantry. In the saloons there were heaters at floor-level, clocks over the cab-doors and lighting from glazed panels above the windows, seen from outside by slim green stained-glass. The ceilings were covered by Alhambrinal panels, lined in two shades of brown, matching the moquette of the seating. The bodies were mounted on E.M.B. bogies, familiar on other systems but not previously in Blackpool. Since they were a lightweight type, the flexible-axle bogies gave better riding qualities. Brush cars could always be distinguished by the chrome flares on each side, and the second ten had the green "V" added at each end. At first they operated on the new Squires Gate & Fleetwood route from Rigby Road depot. It is true that once the platform being loaded with suitcases, the driver wrongly opened the off-side doors and they all fell into to Lytham Road in the path of a following bus! In 1940 the Brush cars were transferred to Bispham depot and operated on North Station & Fleetwood route until 1963. For the 1937 Illuminations, it was decided to create a modern illuminated car, replacing original illuminated De-Luxe car 68. It was in a streamlined style, its profile lined in coloured lights with opaque windows showing the shadows of passengers. It was built upon the oldest B & F crossbench car 141.

1938 – The Finale of The Successful "Five Year Plan"

The new turning loops at Starr Gate and Little Bispham were complete in May and June respectively. The future of the Metropole street track was in the news, and Walter Luff proposed a scheme to include the track on a paved reservation which narrowed the pavements. Nothing materialised until 2011! After the outcry which followed the tramway closures of 1936, it was decided to relay the Marton route, once the work on Lytham Road was completed. It was proposed that single-track would be laid in the centre of Clifton Street, Talbot Road and Abingdon Street to make a terminal loop. Fifteen double-deck cars were to be purchased for the Marton route, and plans were designed by English Electric. These would be a shortened version of the 1934 Balloons, with three-window saloons and 72 seats. When the Second World War broke out in September 1939, none of these developments took place until afterwards. However a modern streamlined fleet had been created to replace old-type cars, except B & F semi-open crossbench cars. In November 1938, a design for its modern equivalent was designed by English Electric. Twelve of these sun-saloons would be built, having wooden reversible seats, half-open windows and a centre folding canvas roof, but they would use equipment from older cars. They were not delivered until the outbreak of War, numbered 10-21, and ironically did become troop-carriers and had to be enclosed! (see details on page 54)

The success of the "Five Year Plan" was shown by 116 streamlined trams, improved facilities for passengers and employees. Fares had not been increased during this time, there had been no redundancies and wages were increased by 11% with 12 paid holidays a year. The public did benefit a 100% better service, and bus operation turned into a profit. Thus Walter Luff had been favoured by modernisation, its achievements gave Blackpool a system to be proud of and carried it forward through the War until the following post-war years!

One of the smart Marton Vambacs seen on Whitegate Drive, with little traffic seen. John Fozard (opposite) New illuminated car 141, promoting the War-effort by 1939. Notice the Spitfire models at each end, and the clock with PRECAUTIONS AIR RAID, & illuminated JOIN YOUR LOCAL A.R.P.

Modernisation of the Marton Route 1947

Once the Second World War was over, the priority for Manager Walter Luff was to proceed with the modernisation of the Marton route. The "Battle for Marton Trams" started in 1946, when Walter Luff presented a report on track renewal and also three alternative forms of transport, and there was a delay in decision. This gave him a chance of promoting the trams: "A tram, which by its sheer frequency and riding qualities, could compete not just with the bus, but with the future competitor the private car." He was determined to show a modern tram on Marton, and therefore a pair of Maley & Taunton resilient-wheel bogies were delivered and fitted to Brush car 303, which was repainted in a cream livery with green flares. At 2300 on 9th April 1946 it went to the Marton route, and when the service cars finished it ran over the worst of the track. The local press described it as "sensational", and BBC made recordings to compare the silence of 303 with the noise of the Standards on rough track. Modern development continued in November with railcoach 208 being fitted with PCC-type VAMBAC equipment and Maley & Taunton bogies. On 19th November 208 in the post-war livery ran over the well-worn rail of the Marton route. The special meeting of the Council was held to consider the future of the Marton route with the shocking track. Fortunately the impression was made by 208's demonstration, and on 8th January 1947 the Council voted 25 to 21 that the Marton route should be retained. The Borough Surveyor was instructed to relay the track immediately. (See 208 on pages 43 & 67, 303 on page 53)

With the relaying of the track, provision was made for the clearance of 8-foot wide cars on the service, showing that Walter Luff wanted modern trams for Marton. The Surveyors Department began work in haste with the worst section at Raikes Parade first. During 1947 the three-minute service was maintained, single-line working being operated between crossovers and using single-line staffs. Experimental 208 & 303 exchanged bogies and equipment, and thus 303 was tried in service amongst the Standards on the Marton route, but its power sliding-doors delayed it on the street route. The introduction of modern trams began in summer 1949, with sun-saloons 10-14 going into service on Marton. While in modern livery they still had their conventional bogies and equipment. In June 1949 sun saloon 21 was fitted with VAMBAC equipment and M & T resilient bogies, and thus became known as a "Marton Vambac". This fitting proceeded through the class in reverse numbers until 10 was reached, and it cost £5,048 each, much less than a new tram. Standards stayed on the South Pier route until 1952. In 1951 the 50th Anniversary of the Marton route was commemorated, with notices in the shelters and Marton Depot was decorated with flags. The local rejoicing confirmed that the route had survived and now had the best trams in the town. Undoubtedly the 12 Marton Vambac cars with their comfortable seats, smooth riding and the brightness of their fluorescent lights, defeated the notion that trams were outdated. When the new Coronations began delivery in 1952, a trial run was made by 305 to Marton depot at 2300 on 6th August, as a demonstration for the Councillors. Walter Luff retired in 1954, and while the Marton route continued in that decade, in Autumn 1960 it was announced that the Squires Gate route would close in 1961 and Marton would follow on 28th October 1962, There was an attempt to save the route, but it had become the final street tramway in Britain, and so it had a closing ceremony with Standards 40, 48, 158 & 159 at Marton depot, and we enthusiasts were told that sadly Marton had now become NOTRAM!

Two Marton Vambacs in original livery passing at Royal Oak junction, while on the South Pier service. The Tower is seen in between them! *John Fozard*

Round Blackpool by Tram

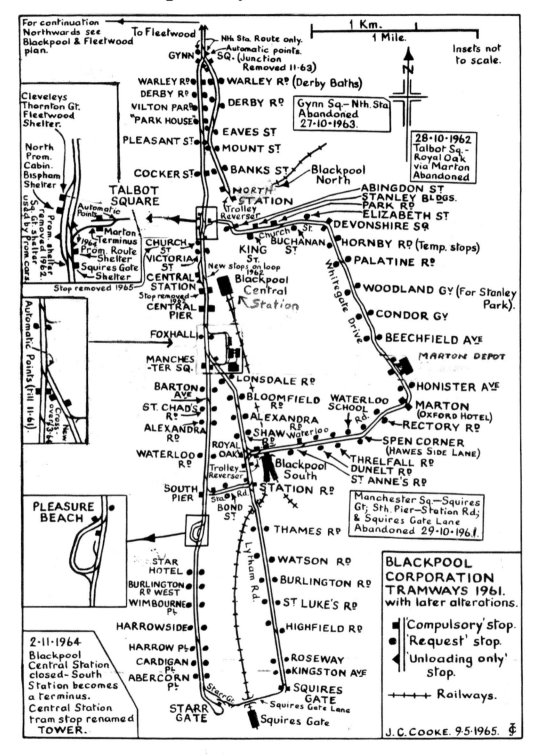

TRAMCAR SERVICES

Cars shown in the tables below are "service" cars - those cars which run with scheduled time cards. Many "specials" are run as required, mainly on Promenade.

SUMMER SEASON 1961

SERVICE NUMBER	DUTY NOS.	ROUTE OPERATED	FREQUENCY	DEPOT	CARS
1	1-9	North Station and Fleetwood	10 minutes	Bispham	9
1	10-13	North Station and Cleveleys	10 minutes	Bispham	4
2	71-83	Starr Gate and Fleetwood	10 minutes	Rigby Road	13
2	22-30	Starr Gate and Thornton Gate	10 minutes	Rigby Road	9
3	51-57	Squires Gate and Bispham	10 minutes	B ispham	7
3	58-63	Squires Gate and Cabin	10 minutes	Rigby Road	6
4	33-44	Talbot Square and Royal Oak	4 minutes	Marton	} 12
4	33-44	Talbot Square and South Pier	12 minutes	Marton	

Total Number of Service Cars: 60

Added to this, as many as 60 or 70 "specials" could be on the road, including cars operating on the Circular Tour, Fleetwood and Cleveleys, Squires Gate and Talbot Square peak hour services.

Last Trams on Converted Routes

LAST CAR	DATE	ROUTE	REPLACEMENT
Standard 154	19th October, 1936	Talbot Square and Layton	} Bus Services 22-23 Marton Depot & Layton.
Unknown	19th October, 1936	Talbot Square and Central Station via Marton	
E.E. r/c/2 268	29th October, 1961	Squires Gate and Cabin	} Bus Service 12 Tram: Harrowside & Cabin.
E.E. r/c/1 201	29th October, 1961	Squires Gate and Bispham	
E.E. r/c/1 205	29th October, 1961	South Pier-Marton	Not immediately replaced
Standard 48	28th October, 1962	Royal Oak - Marton	} Bus Service 26
Standard 159	28th October, 1962	Talbot Square-Marton	
Balloon d.d. 256	27th October, 1963	North Station Cabin	} Bus Service 25A Tram: Tower & Fleetwood.
Brush Car 290	27th October, 1963	North Station and Fleetwood	

Historic Tramway Events 1960 – 2010

75th Anniversary of the tramway 1960

In 1960 the Promenade Tramway reached its 75th Anniversary, since it started in 1885 on the conduit system. The General Manager J. C. Franklin thought it would be a good anniversary to celebrate by restoring four historic trams, which were found in three depots. Fortunately an 1885 ex-conduit car 4 was stood at the back of Bispham depot, having been an overhead-line works-car until 1934. It was driven to Rigby Road Works in February 1960, for rebuilding in the 1885 appearance. In Copse Road depot at Fleetwood was found Dreadnought 59, which had been saved from scrapping in 1934 by a phone call by Manager Walter Luff. One night it was towed back to the Works by an E.E. railcoach, since it had no controller or trolley! Also in the same depot was the only remaining crossbench-car 2 of the B & F Tramroad, which was works-car 127 and driven to the Works. The final one was B &F saloon car 40, which was an Engineering Car, and stood in Rigby Road depot as a rest-room for the staff. When restored and repainted they represented two tramways: 4 & 59 of Blackpool Borough Tramway in red and white, 2 & 40 of Blackpool & Fleetwood Tramroad Company in brown and cream. On 29th September 1960 these cars twice led a procession of eleven cars from Pleasure Beach to Little Bispham, and gave their passengers – except on No.4 - a free ride. Incidentally 4 proclaimed "THIS IS IT" and so was wrongly numbered 1!

This was the climax of the anniversary celebrations, and also marked the conclusion of a successful year's operation. Blackpool had not been slow to see the money-making potential of these attractive tramcars, and so Crossbench car 2 and Dreadnought 59 had been carrying passengers on the Promenade Circular Tour. Box 40 was more suitable for taking passengers to Fleetwood on each Market day. However No.1 was left out of this hectic activity, in case its venerable age should become victim of modern tramway life. After 1960 celebrations were over, the four cars were stored in Marton depot, making occasional sorties for tours, and then Copse Road depot. With the closure of the street routes in 1961-2, it was decided that the Tramway Museum Society at Crich in Derbyshire should be given these historic cars. They left Blackpool in 1963, and 2 & 40 became the first operating trams at the museum. Dreadnought 59 was the Daily Mirror tram each year until 1965, and then went to Crich.

75th Anniversary procession on Central Prom in 1960, with 1, 2, 59, Balcony 40 & Box 40, full of passengers, apart from leading car THIS IS IT!

The Gazette

Centenary of the Tramway 1985

Certainly the return of Dreadnought 59 between 1976 & 1990, always succeeded in attracting passengers for rides along Blackpool Promenade and even to Fleetwoood! 59 was sponsored by Blackpool Civic Trust for the Centenary of the Borough in 1976, and it first stood on display at Foxhall on the Promenade, and then went to Blackpool Technical College for the restoration of the body. On 12th June 1976, Dreadnought 59 appeared on the Tower siding with costumed passengers of Civic Trust to witness the Centenary procession passing on the road. The famous Les Dawson once recorded a programme on the top deck of 59, and it also commenced the first Tram Sunday at Fleetwood in 1985. In this year it was the Centenary of the Promenade Tramway, and consequently 1885 ex-conduit 4 returned to Blackpool, having been restored to its original appearance as a conduit car. Thus it had no trolley and was powered by batteries concealed under the longitudinal saloon seats. On 29th September, car 4 with all of its passengers wearing traditional costumes, led a procession of twenty trams from Talbot Square to Pleasure Beach. Followed by Dreadnought 59, there were thirteen different Blackpool trams, and six from other cities: Edinburgh 35, Hill of Howth 10, Manchester 765, Glasgow 1297, Sheffield 513, Bolton 66, and surprisingly steam tram engine "John Bull" of 1885. Undoubtedly this was the most memorable occasion on the tramway, watched by thousands of people who afterwards took rides. In that year, the newly-restored open-topper 706 was named by the royal "Princess Alice", and can still be seen to this day.

Part of the Centenary procession on 29 September 1985, with Balcony Standard 40, Princess Alice 706 and Pantograph 167, and many others following.

Author

In 1990 two historic cars together at the Pleasure Beach, on a tour for the Fylde Tramway Society.

Author

Centenary of B & F Tramroad 1998

Of the two historic cars of the Tramroad Company, both returned to Blackpool on special occasions. Box 40 first returned from Heaton Park in Manchester, where it had been since 1979 and was more thoroughly restored, in being repanelled, rewired, and it wheels retyred before its arrival in 1988. In traditional livery, 40 was sponsored by local "Fisherman's Friend" and led the Tram Sunday procession in 1988. Seen with Dreadnought until 1990, the contrasting pair provided a reminder of the history when their tramway were merged in 1920. Box 40 returned to NTM Crich in 1991, was an exhibition for a short time and then went into store. However with the Centenary in 1998, 40 returned for restoration in April 1996, and was repainted in traditional livery, complete with "BLACKPOOL & FLEETWOOD ELECTRIC TRAMROAD" in gold letters. To complete this historic Centenary, the N.T.M. completely restored Crossbench car 2 and Pantograph car 167, ready for their return to Blackpool on 22 June 1998. During the short time they were in Blackpool, they were exhibited on depot Open Day. Also 2 & 40 commemorated the opening of the Blackpool & Fleetwood line on 1st July, with crowds of children cheering their arrival at Ash Street, as in 1898. Undoubtedly this was an epic occasion, along with a procession of trams from Pleasure Beach to Fleetwood on 12th July, thus celebrating the survival of the inter-urban tramway for 100 years!

125 Years by Tram 1885 - 2010

With the achievement of reaching 125 years in the history of the Blackpool Tramway, Blackpool Transport and enthusiasts felt that it was recorded by a ceremony on 29th September 2010. Undoubtedly the events of 1985 was a memorable occasion with a twenty tram procession! However in 2010 work was proceeding with the modernisation of the tramway, which would restrict historic trams between Pleasure Beach & Bispham. The Planning Committee agreed that approach would be made to several tramway museums for the loan of historic trams in September 2010. The NTM Crich museum said that it would loan Blackpool Standard 40 and Pantograph 167, also LCC 106, Johannesburg 60 and Leeds 399. However, these did not materialise since Leeds 399 was not ready and 60 was damaged by a tree and returned. All double-deckers were banned from coming, and finally we had Crossbench 2, Pantograph 167 and Oporto 273. Beamish Open Air Museum sent Blackpool open-top 31, which previously came in 1998 and was admired by it restoration from a works-car. Wirral Transport Museum sent Liverpool 762, which appeared safely in August and could be seen along the Promenade for driver training. Heaton Park of Manchester sent 765 for the second time to Blackpool, and it always looked attractive by the sea! However we were disappointed when it was not agreed that East Anglia Transport Museum would exchange its restored Blackpool Marton Vambac 11 in return for a Boat car. Lancashire Transport Trust managed to restore and deliver OMO 8, which I saw on 14 September going into the Works for preparation for the procession.

The passenger's view from 147 in 2010, seeing Pantograph 167 and Crossbench-car 2 here for 125th Anniversary. *Author*

On open-top 31 in the procession, here we are leaving the loop and passing Boat 600, 706 and Coronation 660, waiting to follow. R . P. Fergusson

Before the Centenary Day, as part of the many tours held included trams already in Blackpool, including Stockport 5, Sheffield 513, Bolton 66, Blackpool Box 40, Standard 147 and Coronation 304 which appeared together. Unfortunately Oporto derailed during driver training and was withdrawn from usage, and Pantograph 167 broke down at Bispham on 11 September and had to be towed back to the depot withdrawn. Open Day was a popular event at the depot on Sunday 16 September, with a line-up of many historic trams: 304, 167, partially-rebuilt 143, 31, Box 40, Crossbench 2 & Western Train, including many others inside the depot. When Wednesday 29th arrived, it was disappointing that it was raining, although relief arrived for the procession of eight trams – 2, 40, 31, 147, 600, 706, 660 & OMO 8 – from Pleasure Beach & Bispham. It was fortunate that it took place, at the end of a historic era, with a new generation of articulated trams to follow in 2012!

The procession having returned to the Pleasure Beach, passengers begin to leave 31 and 147. Author

HISTORIC TRAMS FOR THE

1898 Crossbench-car 2 at North Pier on 12 September 2010 on a shuttle-tour.   *Author*

A remarkable line-up on the Pleasure Beach loop in 2010, with Manchester California 765, B & F Box 40 & B & F Crossbench 2.   *Author*

125ᵀᴴ ANNIVERSARY 2010

Bispham central-siding with 2 & 765 during tours in September 2010 and Standard 147 passing showing L plate during driver-training. Bryan Grint

Pantograph 167 and Standard 147 about to reverse at Bispham in 2010 Author

All Tramcar Types 1965 - 2012

In the Centenary Year 1985, Standard 40 and Pantograph 167 at Pleasure Beach while visiting Blackpool

Author

(opposite) 147 Loading passengers at Cleveleys in 2002, newly-restored when returned from U.S.A.

Author

Standards

BUILT: 1923 – 1929 **BUILDER:** Blackpool Corporation Transport Department

BODY: As built, double-deck open-balcony unvestibuled: cars of traditional design and capacity 78 passengers. Seats for 32 were provided in the lower saloon with a combination of longitudinal and transverse cushioned seats and upstairs with 46 wooden transverse seats in the saloon and curved bench seats on the balconies. A four-window saloon with a Tudor-arch effect was inherited from the "Motherwell" cars of 1902, and characterised these cars. Twenty-two new Standards were constructed, beginning with cars 99 and 100 in 1923. In addition, thirty-three cars of older types were constructed by B.C.T. to bring the total of Standard cars up to a maximum of fifty-five. New cars were built as follows:-

99 – 100 built 1923 by B.C.T.	150 – 152 built 1925 by Hurst Nelson
142 – 143 built 1924 by B.C.T.	153 - 155 built 1926 by B.C.T.
144 - 145 built 1925 by B.C.T.	156 - 160 built 1927 by B.C.T.
146 – 149 built by Hurst Nelson	177 built 1929 by B.C.T.

TRUCKS: Preston McGuire equal-wheel bogies, 4ft. 1 in wheel base, 30 in diameter wheels

MOTORS: British Thompson-Houston B 510

BRAKING: Hand-wheel and rheostatic; 147 now fitted with air-brakes.

COLLECTOR: Trolley-boom with 4 inch swivel-head. 147 now fixed-head

DIMENSIONS: Length: 33 ft. 10 in. Height: 16 ft. 7 in. Width: 7 ft. 2 in.

MODIFICATIONS: Certain new Standards were fitted with Hurst Nelson maximum traction bogies at the outset. The first cars were vestibuled in March 1929, and in September of the following year. 159 became the first totally-enclosed car along with 100. 158 was one of a further six cars authorised for totally-enclosing in 1930. Vestibuled open-balcony cars 147, 150, 151, 160, & 177 ran until the war period, when their balconies were enclosed. These replaced cars 46 and 50, which were scrapped after accidents. 158 & 159 were decorated with lights in 1959, and thereafter operated as illuminated cars at night, but during the day as ordinary passenger-cars.

OPERATION: Standards ran on all routes in the town, with exception of the Fleetwood route. In 1935-6 new streamlined "Balloons" replaced Standards on the Gynn Square & Squires Gate via Lytham Road service. Standards were then confined to Layton, Marton, Central Drive and South Pier group of routes, and peak-hour "specials" on the Promenade. Following the abandonment of the Layton and Central Drive routes in October 1936, only fourteen Standards were required for the Marton service during winter season, and those were the all-enclosed type. The starting of WW 11 in 1939 prevented the purchase of fifteen shorter Balloons for the Marton route, and thus Standards remained in service. Following the relaying of this track in 1948, new rolling-stock in the form of sun-saloon "Vambac" cars 10-21 were introduced to the route, replacing Standards. However, it was not until 1952 that the Standards lost their scheduled duties to South Pier, when six railcoaches were transferred from the Promenade duties, after the arrival of the Coronations. 24 Standards were scrapped in Blundell Street depot, and a further six at Thornton Gate sidings in 1958, leaving eight for Promenade use, until their finale by 147, 158 & 159 in 1966. Balcony 40 returned from N.T.M. Crich for the Centenary in 1985. 147 returned from USA in October 2000, fully-restored and launched on 3 April 2002, and remains in Blackpool as a Heritage tram in 2012.

Pantograph 167 in July 1998 outside the North Euston Hotel. *Author*

Pantograph Cars 167 - 176

BUILT: 1928 BUILDER: English Electric , Dick Kerr Works, Preston.

BODY: Single-deck "Pullman" cars, with enclosed platforms, providing rear entrance and exit. Purchased at £2,000 each for use on the Blackpool & Fleetwood route. The design reflects the inter-urban nature of the line, and follows American, rather than British practice. A clerestory roof is a feature of the saloon, which seats 44 on upholstered transverse seats, with two fixed seats on each platform, making a total of 48. A square route-box was originally fitted on the roof at each end, which displayed letters, like "F" for Fleetwood. The notable feature was the pantograph collector by Brecknell, Munro & Rogers, mounted on a tall tower. Car 167 was delivered on Monday 30 July 1928, and the others arrived at intervals thereafter, 174-176 arriving early in 1929.

TRUCKS: Dick Kerr equal-wheel bogies (McGuire type) until 1950, then E.E. 1939-type from Sunsaloons 10 -21, apart from 167 which retains the original ones.

MOTORS: G.E.C. WT 28L: H .P. 40 x 2 (167 has B.T.H. 265 motors)

CONTROLLERS: B . T. H. B 510

BRAKING: Air-wheel brakes by Westinghouse, hand-wheel, rheostatic.

COLLECTOR: Pantograph removed after five years, and replaced by trolley pole with rope.

DIMENSIONS: Length: 40 feet, width: 7ft 6in., platform-entrance: 5ft 6 in.

MODIFICATIONS: Various alterations have taken place structurally since new. The pantograph collector was removed because of sand interfering with the lubrication, and the unsuitability of the overhead line along the Promenade, restricting them to the North Station route. Route-boxes were replaced by indicator-boxes in 1929-30. During 1936-7 they were redesigned to bring them into line with modern trams, by the fitting of platform-doors, larger metal windscreens and curved moulding round the indicator boxes. They were then painted in all-cream livery with green linings. Bogies from 10-21 were fitted to all cars except 167 which became a Permanent Way car in 1954. After a passenger-flow alteration to the body, 176 was scrapped in the same year. Remaining cars were used on the summer-service until 1960. 172 & 175 made the last passenger service at Easter 1961 without their trolley-ropes, in order to use the new trolley-reverser at North Station.

OPERATION: Operating almost exclusively on North Station & Fleetwood service with short-workings to Cleveleys and Thornton Gate, running from Bispham Depot

SITUATION: All these cars were withdrawn from passenger service after Easter 1961. 168 was withdrawn in May 1961, in order to become The Rocket illuminated tram. 174 became the trailer for the Western Train in 1962. 170 became the Works-car in January 1962, and was converted to illuminated frigate H.M.S. Blackpool in April 1965. Preserved 167 returned to Blackpool for the Centenary 1985, for the Tramroad Centenary in 1998 and for the 125th Anniversary in 2010. Restoration of the Frigate took place in 2003-4 and the Western Train in 2009. The Rocket was sited in Gynn Square roundabout and illuminated until 2014.

Pantograph 168 passing Crossbench 2 on a Promenade Circular at Little Bispham in 1960.

R.P. Fergusson

English Electric Railcoaches Series 1. 200 – 224

BUILT: 1933-34

BUILDERS: English Electric Company BODY: Single-deck centre-entrance cars based upon the revolutionary design of prototype 200, which had been originally designed for the overseas market. Under the General Manager Walter Luff's Five Year Plan of Modernisation, 24 cars like 200 were ordered. They were designed to replace the old B & F ex-Company saloon cars, and offered new standards of passenger comfort. 48 transverse, reversible and cushioned seats were provided, floor heaters were fitted and an electric clock in each saloon. The driver was seated in his own cab, while the safety of passengers was ensured by folding doors on the platform. Each saloon had sliding-opening sunshine-roof panels.

TRUCKS: English Electric equal-wheel bogies; 4ft.wheelbase.

MOTORS: English Electric 305 H.P. 57 x 2

CONTROLLERS: E.E. type Z4

BRAKING: Westinghouse air-wheel, hand-wheel and rheostatic.

COLLECTOR: Trolley-boom mounted on a tower. 200 was fitted with a pantograph at Preston and briefly at Blackpool. Cars fitted with a 6 inch wheel on swivel-head trolleys, when running from Marton Depot.

DIMENSIONS: Length: 43 ft. 3 in. over fenders. Width: 7ft. 6 in.

FURTHER NOTES: With remarkably few changes, these cars gave staunch service for over thirty years, from 1934 until general withdrawal in 1963, with the closure of the North Station route. Car 200 was delivered in June 1933 and 224 in February 1934. Only cars 214 and 224 had their sliding "sunshine" roofs removed.

Two railcoaches passing at Foxhall Square, the Tower dominating the scene.   Author's Collection

208 at Rigby Road depot in April 1949, about to start its first tour for LRTL members.

John. H. Meredith

OPERATION: Railcoaches were operated on all routes and from three depots, and latterly they provided the basic service on North Station and Squires Gate routes. Each depot had its allocation.

SITUATION: 206 was the first car to be scrapped on 22 September 1961, after a collision with a Coronation at Gynn Square. This series reduced because of conversion to bus operation of the three tram routes by 1963. 224 became a Permanent Way car in October 1964, but was restored to service in May 1965, being an only Series I in operation. 221 became Engineering car on 21 April 1965, and 220 was stored on Blundell Street depot. In 1972 these three became OMO cars: 3 - 224 (610), 4 - 220 (608), 5 - 221 (609) today preserved at N.T.M...

VAMBAC RAILCOACH 208

The car in December 1946 became the first Blackpool "Vambac" car, being experimentally fitted with the multi-notch accelerator in the base of is tower, and enclosed by ventilating masking. Also it was fitted with distinct amber glass above its windscreen, to provide the driver with sun-shading.

TRUCKS: Maley & Taunton HS 44 with track brakes.

MOTORS: Crompton Parkinson C 92

H.P. : 45 x 4

CONTROLLERS: Crompton Parkinson "VAMBAC".

OPERATION: Ran from Marton Depot on this route after initial trials.

SITUATION: Scrapped at Marton Depot in March 1963

Open Boat Cars 225 – 236 Now 600 – 607

BUILT: 1934-35

BUILDER: English Electric, Preston

BODY: Designed by General Manager Walter Luff, these cars were intended to have all advantages of the Toastracks without the disadvantages of the running-boards along the sides. Consequently they have centre-entrance, over which is a canopy supporting the trolley tower and containing four indicators and signal bells. The open saloons have sides reaching to a seat-top level, and 56 seats wooden-slatted and reversible. The body is of composite construction with an under-frame of rolled-steel sections, teak framework, and steel panels. 225 being the trial car, differs in having lower sides. Flares at each end are lined with beading, and the platforms have half-height doors.

TRUCKS: English Electric equal-wheel, 4ft. wheelbase

MOTORS: E.E. 327

H.P. 40 x 2

CONTROLLERS: E.E. D.B. 1 on cars 225, 226, 236. B.T.H. B.18 cars 227 – 235 Subsequently all were fitted with E.E. Z 6, from railcoaches. BRAKING: Westinghouse air-wheel, rheostatic, hand-wheel.

COLLECTOR: Trolley boom and swivel-head until 1962, now fixed-head.

DIMENSIONS: 42 ft. 4 in. in length, width 7 ft. 6 in.

MODIFICATIONS: In 1958 car 227 was fitted with a light windscreen, and all followed until 1959. By 1990, these were replaced by twin-windscreens of toughened glass. Pantographs were fitted to 602 and 604 in 1992, but were unsuitable for passengers, whose clothes were stained. Trolleys were restored.

OPERATION: All these cars were based at Marton Depot and operated the Circular Tour and Promenade "specials". When it closed in October 1962, four Boats went to Blundell St. Depot and eight to Bispham Depot, where they operated Promenade Circulars and "specials". In 1964 eight transferred to Rigby Rd. Depot.

SITUATION: In April 1968 229, 231, 232, 234 were scrapped in Blundell St. Depot as surplus. In 1971, 226 (601) went to San Francisco for the British Trade Festival and then to Rio Vista Museum in California. In 1976 228 (603) went to Philadelphia for U.S.A. Bi-Centennial Celebrations, and gave city-centre tours on 5ft. 3 in. gauge track. It was returned in 1978, disused and departed permanently to San Francisco in 1985, where it is operated by MUNI with the international fleet. In 1986, 606 operated at the Glasgow Garden Festival, in 2000 went to Trolleyville U.S.A. in exchange for Standard 147. It is now in Washington Transport Museum. Today three Boats remain in the Blackpool Heritage Fleet: 600 (225), 227, 230. N.T.M. Crich operate 236 (607). 605 first went to Beamish and then was sold to MUNI of San Fransico and joined 228 there, as 233!

Three Boats lined-up for Circular Tours in Talbot Square in 1959, & Boat 225 (600) travelling down Squires Gate Lane on a Circular Tour.   *Author*

Former Open-Top Balloons 237 – 249, now 700 - 712

BUILT: 1934

BUILDER: English Electric, Preston.

BODY: Introduced by Walter Luff to replace the Dreadnoughts, these cars were a modern version of the traditional seaside open-topper. The body and bogies were manufactured in Preston and the traction equipment in Bradford. Steel shutter blinds could close the staircases during the poor weather, and make the car a single-decker. Entrance to the platform was by two-piece folding doors. Each saloon seated 20 on upholstered transverse seats, while on the open-top deck, 54 teak wooden slatted seats were provided, and bench seats provided at each end, totalling 94. The body has a teak frame, built on an under-frame of welded rolled steel. The trolley was supported by a gantry arch in the centre of the upper deck.

TRUCKS: E.E. equal-wheel bogies, 4 ft. 9 in. wheelbase, wheels 27 in. diameter

MOTORS: E.E. 305 H.P. 57 x 2

CONTROLLERS: E.E. Z 6. Designed to increase the running-speed of double-deckers from the 24 mph for Promenade and street running to 35 mph on reservation, using 8th notch field-shunt position.

BRAKING: Westinghouse air-wheel, rheostatic 8-notches, hand-wheel.

COLLECTOR: Trolley boom – now only seen on 706, pantographs on the others.

DIMENSIONS: Length 42 ft. 3 in., width 7 ft 6in., centre-doorway 4ft 6in.

MODIFICATIONS: Car 237 was delivered on 6 February 1934 and displayed at Talbot Square as 226 with Boat 225. It was renumbered when 12 Boats were ordered 225 – 236, and thirteen open-toppers 237 – 249. Certainly 237 had a more vertical front, which became more sloped on the others. During the war, in 1941 and 1942, the top decks of these cars were enclosed in the style of 250 – 263, and the end bench seats were removed, reducing the capacity to 84. These could always be identified without the windscreen hoods, a more flat roof, and the thinly-upholstered seats on the upper-deck. These were subsequently replaced by upholstered seats, and the padded bench seats restored at each end, giving 94 seats. Today, many fixed bus-type seats have been fitted, half forward and backwards.

SITUATION: In July 1980, following the collision between 705 & 706, 705 was scrapped in 1982, but 706 was rebuilt in the open-top condition for Centenary in 1985, when it was named "PRINCESS ALICE" by the Queen's aunt. Unfortunately it was fitted with a short roof with a pantograph, but this was replaced by a trolley. In 2003 it was repainted in the original style and windscreen hoods fitted. At Easter 1997, prototype 700 was rebuilt with twin-indicators and windscreens in 1942 form, with the wartime green livery and a trolley pole. In 2003 the windscreen hoods were fitted. 707 & 709 (718 & 724) were rebuilt with flat fronts, single-windscreen, new fitted hopper-windows and fixed seating. 700, 707, 709, & 711, now have wider platform and automatic doors, to help boarding.

In 1961 pedestrians watching 247 (710) using the trolley-reverser outside the Odeon, on a tea-time special for Bispham. (opposite) In its original style, a Balloon is seen passing The Palace in the Thirties. *Author*

Double-Deck Balloons 250 – 263, Now 713 – 726

BUILT: 1934 – 35 **BUILDER**: English Electric, Preston.

BODY: Similar in specification to the open-toppers, the first of these cars was on exhibition in the English Electric Works in Preston on 3 December 1934, along with modern cars for Sunderland, Belfast, Leeds and trolleybuses for Bradford. 250 arrived in Blackpool on 10 December 1934 and most of the fourteen Balloons had been delivered by Easter 1935, each costing £3,500. They had seating for 84 passengers, with 20 in each saloon and 44 on the upper deck. Heating was provided by thermostatically-controlled radiators through grills at floor level. Ventilation was by half-drop windows and in the upper saloon there were two 6 ft. sliding roof panels. Ceilings comprised Alhambrinal panels, and lighting was provided on each side of the roof, behind curved glass covered with art-deco style pattern.

MODIFICATIONS: These cars were distinguished from 237 – 249 by the centre arch over the roof, which supports the trolley and allows the open sunshine roofs to slide underneath. 250 was fitted with fluorescent lighting in 1946. Re-fitting with single indicator display using fibreglass moulding, began with car 257 in June 1955, and proceeded until finally 722 (259) in 1980. All cars were increased to 94 seating, by adding bench seats at each end of the upper saloon. Sunshine roofs were removed, along with the trolley-arch, culminating with 722 in 1980.

OPERATION: Balloons of both series operated on Squires Gate service in summer and winter until 1951, when all double-deckers were withdrawn from winter service. Subsequently, operation was confined to the Squires Gate service in summer until 1961, when the route was converted to buses. In 1958 Balloons operated to Fleetwood for the first time, when the track was fitted with check-rail. In 1971 they operated Fleetwood & Starr Gate service for the first time during summer season, and this continued until 2009, only to Little Bispham in 2010.

SITUATION: 725 & 714 were rebuilt as Jubilee cars 761 & 762 (see page 58). 717 was fully-restored to its original condition 2008, and is now in Heritage fleet. Cars 713, 718, 719, 720 & 724 have widened platforms and automatic doors and warning to passengers.

E. E. Railcoaches Series 2 264 – 283 Then 611 - 620

BUILT: On 28th January 1935, a tender for a further twenty railcoaches was accepted from the English Electric Company and these cars became 264 –283. In specification they are the same as the cars of the first series, with the exception that they were fitted with the improved Z6 controllers.

MODIFICATION: Half of these railcoaches 272-281 were rebuilt as towing-cars for the trailers, which arrived in 1960 (see page 50) In 1965 the remaining railcoaches were having the sliding sunshine roofs removed, which gave them a flat roof. During the winter of 1963, they were also fitted with fan-heaters mounted centrally over the entrance to each saloon. A new three-colour livery was adopted: cream panels, green above them and an orange tower.

OPERATION: Originally operating Starr Gate & Fleetwood route, they were replaced by Coronations in 1953. Then they were mostly allocated to Marton and Rigby Road depots, and used on the Squires Gate route until 1961 and Marton route until 1962. On the latter route were cars 265, 266, 269, 282 & 283, which were fitted with swivel-head trolleys. They transferred to the Fleetwood route in October 1962 and were used on Fleetwood & Cleveleys local service during winter 1963, with fixed trolleys.

SITUATION: In 1966, 264 was rebuilt with the towing-car appearance and panelled in ICI plastic. In 1968, 618 was rebuilt with a longer body and tapering ends, now seating 56. This started the appearance of the OMO cars. In 1972 (269) was then rebuilt to become the first OMO (see opposite).

270 on Lytham Road bound for Little Bispham, seen with a Squires Gate car, both in the Fifites livery.
Author's Collection

OMO 5 at Fleetwood Ferry in February 1976, newly fitted with a Brecknell Willis power-collector.

Author

Railcoaches Became Omos 1 - 13

MODIFICATIONS: Commencing with 616, the body was lengthened by a tapered platform at each end, making it 49 feet. Entrances were at the front, while the centre doors were retained as exit. Thus the driver position was on the right-hand side, and the controller had to be used with the right hand. Saloons were fitted with back-to-back fixed seats and new windows with "hopper" ventilators, and a through centre aisle with steps down to centre doors. The roof tapered to the single indicator at each end. The initial livery was sunshine yellow with a maroon roof. Bogies were rebuilt with Metalastik suspension, starting with OMO 10 in April 1975, which inaugurated a new red and cream livery for these cars.

1972: 1 – 616, 2 – 620, 3 – 610, 4 – 608, 5 – 609.   **1975:** 10 – 614, 11 – 615, 12 - 611.

1973: 6 – 617, 7 – 619.   **1976:** 13 – 618.

1974: 8 – 612, 9 – 613   All became red and cream in livery.

OPERATION: OMOs went into service on the Starr Gate & Fleetwood route in 1972, and throughout the year provided the basic fleet, until the new Centenary trams began to replace them in 1984. They were deemed to be more economical with a crew of one, and had a capacity of 48 seated + 16 standing. However they were not the most popular trams, and became known by the crews as "coffins".

SITUATION: The use of the OMOs ceased in February 1993, with 5. 11 was used for trials with bogies for new articulated cars. OMO 7 was rebuilt in the form of Vanguard crossbench car 619, and is now at Heaton Park. OMO 5 is in store at Clay Cross N.T.M., and OMO 8 is owned by L.T.T. and appeared in the 125th Anniversary procession in 2010.

Trailer Towing-Cars 272 – 281 Now 671 - 680

BUILT: 1935 **BUILDER:** E.E. **REBUILT:** 1959-61 B.C.T.

BODY: 276 & 275 were rebuilt in 1957-8 as twin-car unit. This made its inaugural run to Fleetwood on 9 April 1958, after extensive test and Transport Ministry inspection. Based on experience gained with this unit, ten new trailers were ordered from M.C.W. and railcoach reconstruction began in 1959. In appearance they resembled the Coronations, using aluminium panels and fibre-glass for the roof and mouldings. Lightweight electronic folding-doors were fitted, and lights in the driver's cab indicated when they were open. Curved roof-windows were rubber-mounted, thus flush with the roof, while single-indicators were surmounted by "Progress Twin-car" panel. The saloons were lightened by the use of laminated panels. Automatic couplings were fitted at each end. They appeared in service as follows:-

1960: 276, 272, 277, in summer months, and 280.

1961: 279, 273, 278, 275 (converted from trailer in March), 274. All cars were finished in all-cream livery with green lining at first.

TECHNICAL DETAILS: as for E. E. railcoaches series 1 & 2.

MODIFICATIONS: Cars 281 & T1 permanently coupled in 1963, with driver's cab fitted in the trailer, controls from 281, and seats from T1 making the capacity 53 + 61. Thus the twin-car was reversible on crossovers. Air-hoses were removed from the ends and livery became half green and cream. Seven sets were completed including 677 & 687 in 1970. Upon overhaul in 1969, 676 lost its sunshine roof and rear indicators. 675 retained its sunshine roof until 1980, when removed along with roof windows.

OPERATION: Prototype operated Coastal Tour at first, general "specials" between Starr Gate & Little Bispham or Fleetwood. In October 2003 twin-cars had to take-over main service from Balloons temporarily

SITUATION: In winters 1970-1, 678, 679 & 680 operated separately, and permanently from September 1972. 678 first fitted with Brecknell Willis pantograph in 1975. New bus route liveries were introduced in 2003. 677 became under-frame of Western Train locomotive in 2008, and 687 was redundant. All withdrawn from service in 2011.

A busy scene in Fleetwood with twin-cars 672-682 passing 684 pushed by 674.   *John Fozard*

A Historic scene as the first trailer T1- towed by 677 - is handed over by MCW to Blackpool Transport, and Manager J.C. Franklin is at front right. *The Gazette*

Trailer Cars T1 – T 10, Now 681- 690

BUILT: 1960 BUILDER: Metropolitan Cammel-Weymann Ltd.

BODY: Single-deck, centre-entrance, two saloons seating 66 on transverse reversible upholstered seats. Lightweight construction, use of aluminium-panelling and fibreglass mouldings. Half-drop ventilators in second and fourth windows, and electronic folding platform doors. The saloon has a pleasing finish with linoleum floor coverings, ceiling panels in patterned Alhambrinal, and window framings in aluminium. Roof windows are provided and strip-lighting is fitted next to these. T1 was delivered on 16 July 1960, connected to 677 for presentation by MCW, and used for inaugural run on 25 July. Delivery continued until T9 & T10 arrived in January 1961.

TRUCKS: Maley & Taunton 27 in. equal-wheel bogies with 5 ft. 6 in. wheelbase, outside frame, hornwayless, and rubber-springing.

BRAKING: air-wheel to all wheels, separate hand-brake in trailer.

DIMENSIONS: length: 43ft. 10 in., width: 7ft. 6 in., height: 9ft. 11 in.

MODIFICATIONS: T1 linked with 281 in 1963 and has a waist-height partition of driver's cab. T2-T7 had a complete partition and seats reduced to 61. Headlights were fitted to new front-end of the trailers. New half green and cream livery was introduced.

SITUATION: 688 was scrapped in 1982, 689 & 690 were scrapped in 1989 at Bradford Transport Museum, after their trial by G.E.C. at Kearsley. 687 withdrawn after 677 rebuilt as Loco, 2008. Remaining twin cars preserved for museums and two for Heritage fleet here.

The saloons of a Brush car in 1963, showing chrome fittings and side lights over the windows and with sliding doors.   *Author*

Brush Cars 284–303 Now 621–638

BUILT: 1937 **BUILDER;** Brush Company, Loughborough

BODY: Single-deck saloon body with centre entrance and change in appearance over the English Electric railcoaches. These cars were fitted with air-operated sliding doors by G.D. Peters of Slough, which could be operated also by driver. Forty-eight cushioned reversible seats were provided in the saloons, and two folding seats were provided on the platforms, making the total 50. Since the platform seats were an insurance risk, they were soon removed. The driver had a pedestal seat in each cab. Stainless steel beading on the side panels provided a streamlined appearance, together with painted flares on each end. A Sunbeam sliding roof was fitted in each saloon and finished in Alhambrinal. All the windows were Widney winding full-drop types. Saloon lighting was provided in panels above the windows at each side, and these showed from the outside through green glass. The floor-covering was two-colour linoleum and tubular heaters were fitted at each side. Square clocks were above the driver's cab door in each saloon.

TRUCKS: E.M.B. hornless equal-wheel bogies, 4 ft. 3 in. wheelbase 27 in. wheels. These bogies were designed for a low-loading car, with the side frames swept up over the axle-boxes, which were mounted on the long laminated springs.

MOTORS: Crompton Parkinson C162 (now E.E.305) H.P. 57 x 2

CONTROLLERS: Allen West CTJ (replaced by E.E. Z4)

BRAKING: Air-wheel E.M.B. rheostatic and hand-wheel.

COLLECTOR: Trolley-boom, replaced by pantograph.

DIMENSIONS: Length 42 ft. 3 in., width 7 ft 6 in.

MODIFICATIONS: All cars were fitted with single-indicators at each end, beginning with 288 in 1958, and ending with 284 (621) in 1980. All cars had the sliding sunshine roofs removed, after transfer to Rigby Road in October 1963, and air-sliding doors were replaced by folding doors. Fan heaters were fitted in the saloons in winter 1963, original floor heaters had been disused for some time. Car 301 had fluorescent lighting in 1947. All cars were fitted with E.E. motors and controllers from scrapped railcoaches. 638 (302) was rebuilt for one-man operation with a front door, and in all-cream livery 1970-3, but was withdrawn and scrapped in 1984.

OPERATION: Initially operated from Rigby Road depot, until transferred to Bispham Depot in 1940. Mainly used on the North Station & Fleetwood route, some Promenade duties, Squires Gate & Bispham from 1959 to 1961. From 1964 Starr Gate & Fleetwood.

SITUATION: 624 & 628 became permanent-way works car from 1971. 635 (298) preserved for N.T.M. restoration in 1974. 633 was rebuilt in 2001 as illuminated trawler CEVIC FD241. Only 631 is now in the local BTS Heritage fleet, twelve others are preserved!

VAMBAC BRUSH CAR 303 An experimental car demonstrated on Marton route in 1946, and equipped with VAMBAC equipment in 1953. However retained at Bispham depot subsequently.

TRUCKS: Maley & Taunton H.S. 44 without track brakes.

MOTORS: Crompton Parkinson C92 H.P. 45 x 4

CONTROLLERS: Crompton Parkinson VAMBAC equipment.

BRAKING: Air-disc, remote-control rheostatic, hand-disc.

OPERATION: 303 operated from Bispham depot on occasional use on North Station & Fleetwood and Starr Gate & Cleveleys. Taken to Marton Depot early in 1963 for scrapping.

Brush "Vambac" 303 in Bispham depot yard 1959, note the M & T bogies and ventilators for the accelerator-equipment over the platform.   *Author*

Sunsaloons & Marton Vambacs 10 – 21

BUILT: 1939 **BUILDER:** English Electric, Preston.

BODY: These cars were intended as a modern version of the old B. & F. Crossbench cars which they were intended to replace. Although modern in external appearance, representing the ultimate in pre-war design, they were built cheaply for summer use only. Old electrical equipment was used, including B.T.H. B 265C motors from cars 62 – 68 and Marton Box-cars 27, 29, 30 & 32, while the E.E. DB1 controllers were possibly obtained from other systems. Features included wooden reversible-seating, half-glazed windows, half-height doors, roller-shutter roof, low-lighting and no partition between saloons and driver's cab. The first car was delivered on 14 August 1939, and passengers soon complained about the draughts. Although such cars were not expected to be used in winter, upon the outbreak of the W.W.11, troops were carried by them from Squires Gate to Rossall for training. These trams were known as "cattle trucks", and in 1942 all windows were fully-glazed, roof filled-in, full doors fitted and partition completed. Women drivers insisted to be exclusive!

TRUCKS: English Electric equal-wheel, 4 ft. wheelbase.

MOTORS: B.T.H. B265C

H.P.: 35 x 2

CONTROLLERS: E.E. DB 1

COLLECTOR: Trolley-boom with fixed-head, later swivel-head on Marton route.

DIMENSIONS: Length: 44 ft., width: 7 ft. 6 in.

Sun Saloon 15 in 1941, with roof windows painted over and headlights too, full-length doors and partitions at the end of the saloons.　　　　　　　　　　　　　　　　*M. J. O'Connor NTM*

The scene at Royal Oak on the last day of operation there – 28 October 1962 – with 15 going down and 17 leaving the terminus.   *Peter Fitton*

POST-WAR RECONSTRUCTION

BODY: Sunsaloons continued until 1948, when 10 – 15 were improved with cushioned seats, fluorescent lighting on a new roof panel, completed partitions and placed into service on the newly-relaid Marton route. This continued until 15 went into service on Marton in 1949. Externally the cars were finished in a striking livery of green and cream with green flares on each side and green "V" at each end. Late in 1949 car 21 appeared like the others, but with "VAMBAC" equipment and M & T bogies, thus silent running. Work continued in reverse order to 10, when the twelve Marton Vambacs replaced the Standards. A further six railcoaches should have followed, but the new 25 Coronations 1952-4 needed attention!

TRUCKS: Maley & Taunton HS44 bogies, resilient wheels, 6 ft 0 in. wheelbase.

MOTORS: Crompton Parkinson VAMBAC (Variable Automatic Multinotch Braking and Acceleration Control)

BRAKING: Air-disc, remote-control rheostastic, hand-disc.

OPERATION: Intended for Promenade seasonal use, until the war changed their situation into troop-carriers. Post-war a new role arrived in becoming modern-equipped trams for the Marton route, from 1952 to 1962 when the route was closed on 28 October 1962.

SITUATION: All these cars were broken-up in Marton depot, except 11 survived when it was hired for a final tour with the historic cars in January 1963. 11 was completely restored in 2005 at Carlton Colville, East Anglia Transport Museum, it also visited Beamish Museum in County Durham for operation in September 2011.

Coronations 304–328 then 641- 664

BUILT: 1952-4 **BUILDER:** Charles Roberts of Horbury.

BODY: Single-deck centre-entrance car seating 56 passengers on traverse cushioned seats. Of very handsome appearance, these cars followed the pre-war pattern in having two saloons with centre entrance, which subsequently precluded one-man operation. The unladen weight of 19 tons made them expensive to operate, leading to broken axles at an early stage. However these cars appeared as the ultimate in British tramcar development, with their fluorescent lighting, comfortable seating, glass-panelled roof, Alhambrinal coloured panels, electro-pneumatic sliding doors and "VAMBAC" control equipment. The equipment of 304 was demonstrated at the Festival of Britain 1951 along with a bogie, and a plaque commemorated this. Car 304 was delivered to Blackpool on 5 June 1952 and was first driven from North Pier to Pleasure Beach by the Mayor and comedian Jimmy Edwards. Delivery was completed when 328 arrived on 7 January 1954.

TRUCKS: Maley & Taunton HS 44, equal-wheel bogie, resilient wheels, 6 ft. wheelbase with braking-disc and track-brake shoes.

MOTORS: Crompton Parkinson C. 92 x 4 H.P. 45 x 4

CONTROLLERS: Crompton Parkinson "VAMBAC" accelerator and braking.

BRAKING: Remote-control rheostatic, magnetic track-brakes, air-brakes, hand-brakes.

COLLECTOR: Trolley-pole originally with 6" swivel-head, replaced by fixed-head.

DIMENSIONS: Length: 50 feet, width: 7 ft. 11 in., height: 10 ft.

(above) Coronations 304 and 660 on a F.T.S. Tour at the Cabin in 2005.   *David Butterworth*

(opposite) Coronation 304 brought by Pickfords to Rigby Road depot in 1952, showing NORTH STATION BLACKPOOL on its indicators!   *The Gazette*

MODIFICATIONS: Various features – chrome lining, sliding standee-windows – were removed because of rusting, and the glass roof panels were plated over because they were leaking. Steel side panels were replaced by aluminium, to reduce weight and rusting. In 1961 the coloured Alhambrinal panels were painted over, and the livery was simplified to all-cream with one centre green-band. In 1964, an attempt to reduce maintenance costs and increase reliability resulted in 323 having "Vambac" equipment removed and replaced by E.E. Z6 controllers, using electric-braking for service stops. 328 and 310 followed in 1965, and their fleet livery became half-green and half-cream with orange tower. The resistances were positioned under the tower, providing air-flow cooling. A further ten Coronations followed; 306, 327, 324, 318, 326, 322, 325, 321, 320, and 319 in February 1970. Fluorescent lighting was removed and replaced by light bulbs, thus reducing their original appearance.

OPERATION: Starr Gate and Fleetwood & Thornton Gate until 1963, seasonal until 1970.

SITUATION: The scrapping process started with 313 in 1968, the "Vambac" cars followed, and then the re-equipped cars, completed by 1975. Three have survived: 304 has the VAMBAC equipment and returned for restoration on the "Salvage Squad" TV programme in 2003-4. 660 (324) was retained by the BTS to be used for "Specials", and now in Heritage Fleet with 304. 663 (327) has returned to BTS for restoration, after much ownership in many places.

(left) 761 at Fleetwood Ferry advertising Wilkinsons Supermarkets in 2004. (right) 762 in the same location in green and cream fleet livery, 1984. *Author*

Jubilee Cars 761 & 762

BUILT: 761 - 1979, 762 – 1982 **BUILDER:** Blackpool Borough Transport

BODY: Originally Balloons 725 & 714 were stored in Blundell Street depot, and it was decided to rebuild them to a new design with a front entrance and exit, thus to be operated like OMOs with a crew of one. In the Works, complete reconstruction of 725 body involved the moving of the stairs to each end, thus filling the centre entrance and platform. Complete new end sections were built elsewhere and were added to the body, thus making 761 longer than a Balloon. New longer window sections were fitted flush with the body, thus changing its original appearance. However 761 with 98 seats was found to be slow-loading and unloading through the front entrance. Thus with the construction of 762, a new centre exit and adjacent stairs reduced the seating to 90 and improved passenger-flow. It was surprising that 761 was not rebuilt accordingly. The original plan was to so rebuild the Balloon fleet.

TRUCKS: Blackpool Transport 5 ft. 6 in. wheelbase and Metalistic suspension.

MOTORS: E.E. 305 **H.P.:** 57 x 2

CONTROLLERS: Brush "Chopper" control – operated by lever.

BRAKING: "Chopper" controls air-braking, hand-wheel.

COLLECTOR: Pantograph – originally mini-size on 761.

DIMENSIONS: Length: 46 feet, Width: 7 ft. 6 in., wheelbase: 22ft. 4 in.

OPERATION: These cars have been used on the Starr Gate & Fleetwood service throughout the year, with only driver in winter and joined by conductor in summer.

SITUATION: 761 & 762 were withdrawn on 6 November 2011, 762 has gone to NTM Crich for service in 2012, 761 was stored at Fleetwood by Friends of Fleetwood Trams, then in 2013 returned to Rigby Road Depot for future restoration.

Centenary Cars 641 - 648

BUILT: 1984 – 1988 **BUILDER:** East Lancashire Coachbuilders, Blackburn.

BODY: It was decided in 1982, following the completion of 762, that the replacement of the OMOs should be by ten single-deckers, built by East Lancs. The dimensions would follow the size of the Coronations, and 660 with wooden corner-frames was tested for clearance. The body of 641 left the Blackburn works on 17 April 1984, was weighed 10.5 tonnes at the brewery, and with the bogies would weigh 17.5 tonnes. This new car was a more modern appearance with front entrance and nearer exit, to facilitate driver's vision. On the roof was a large 4-sided advertisement box surmounted by a tapering-tower for pantograph. In the saloon there was fixed seating for 54, facing the centre of the car and some longitudinal seats. Capacity was 74 with 20 standing passengers. On 642-8 seating was 52 and had no advert-box and a different tower. 641 later conformed like the others.

TRUCKS: Blackpool Transport new-frames 5 ft. 6 in wheelbase and Metalistic suspension.

MOTORS: E.E. 305 H.P. 57 x 2

CONTROLLERS: Brush "Chopper" control, operated by lever.

BRAKING: "Chopper" control air-braking, and hand-wheel.

COLLECTOR: Pantograph

DIMENSIONS: Length: 51 ft. 6 in., Width: 8 ft. 2 in., Height: 9 ft. 4 in.

OPERATION: The first trial run for 641 took place: on Promenade 6 June, Fleetwood on 8 June, and entered service on 6 July 1984. The Centenary cars operated the Starr Gate & Fleetwood service throughout the year until 2011, when they were withdrawn.

SITUATION: A second Centenary car appeared in 1985, equipped with G.E.C. equipment and Maley & Taunton bogies, numbered 651. Subsequently in 1988, G.E.C. sold the body to B.T.S. and it was re-equipped and renumbered 648. Rebuilding the Centenaries started with 642 in 1999, replacing "hopper" windows, flooring and moquette. 643 – 647 were rebuilt at the front and all had raised upper sides. 641 was rebuilt as stated in 2000, and the final car was 648, retaining its original appearance. Thus 648 will remain in B.T.S. Heritage fleet from 2012.

648 seen at Thornton Gate in 2007, advertising the new VUE Cinema in Cleveleys. Today 648 is in traditional green and cream livery.

Author

Flexity 2 Cars 001 – 016

BUILT: 2011 – 2012 **BUILDER:** BOMBARDIER

BODY: Five-section double-ended articulated cars, with four doors, double in second and fourth body-sections and single doors at each end. Seating for 74, with double back-to-back pairs, side-seating near to doors and tip-up single seats near to spaces for wheelchairs. Roof- mounted lighting, large windows with opening-tops, non-slip flooring near doors, many yellow vertical hand-rails and strap-hangers with bells for signalling.

TRUCKS: Equal-wheel, resilient-wheels, track-brakes.

MOTORS: 163 hp x 4

SPEED: 43.5 mph, can be restricted to 30 mph.

BRAKING: Electronic braking and track-brakes.

COLLECTOR: Centrally-mounted pantograph.

DIMENSIONS: Length: 105 ft 8 in, width: 8ft 8 in, height: 11ft 3 in.

OPERATION: Starr Gate – Fleetwood, Starr Gate – Cleveleys services.

SITUATION: The first car 001 appeared from the new depot on 8th September 2011 with an official party on South Promenade. Others were delivered at intervals. Driver-training took place, and the new service to Fleetwood started at Easter 2012.

(opposite) 003 in the centre-track of Works, between six pairs of jacks, and close-up of a Flexity 2 bogie. (above) 001 seen on driver's training at Little Bispham boarding-platform in February 2012. (below) A view of 001's long saloon, showing its 74 seats and space for 148 standing passengers, with many yellow hand-rails with bells. Also there are folding seats and vertical pads for leaning on. Passengers are now warned: "Mind the doors, Hold tight please".

Author

Illuminated Trams

During the rebuilding of the Western Train in January 2008, showing the original 1962 wooden-frame, together with new metal-panelling and under-frame and bogies from 677. Author

(left) 733-734 in the Body-shop completed and showing its sponsors. (right) Its first excursion to Fleetwood in Pharos Street on 14 May 2009. R. P. Fergusson

Illuminated trawler 737 named CEVIC FD 241, sponsored by Fisherman's Friend, and built on under-frame and with running-equipment of Brush-car 633. (right) Originally frigate HMS Blackpool, built from 170 in 1965, rebuilt in 2003 and changed its appearance with straight saloon and superstructure above. Also rewired to 24 volt A/c for safety.   Author

Western Train seen in 2011, keeping its original appearance with sponsor ABC WEEKEND TELEVISION, but voltage changed to 24 volt A/c, doors and seating improved.   Bryan Grint

The Tramcar Depots

Since there have been six tram depots in the past, today there are two: Rigby Road depot of 1935 and Starr Gate depot for the 16 Flexity 2 cars and maintenance-works in 2012. All the other depots have disappeared, apart from Copse Road depot in Fleetwood, which will remain as a car salesroom.

Bundell Street, Princess Street, Blackpool.

BUILT: 1884-85 **CAPACITY:** 45 **TRACKS:** 5

SERVICES WORKED: Before l935 Promenade and Squires Gate services, during 1939-1944 operated the Marton route, and 1963 Promenade "specials".

CARS: A wide range of cars from conduit cars in 1885 to new Streamliners in 1933. In post-war years vintage trams were stored there and Standards broken-up until 1954.

HISTORY: Open for ten conduit cars in 1885, extended in 1894 and in 1896 for additional cars. In 1898 came the final extension to its full size, when the roof was raised for the overhead wires. This was the main running-shed until the opening of the new central depot in 1935, after which Blundell St. Depot became largely a store. In post-war years, following break-up of many trams by 1954, the pits were filled-in and it was used as a bus garage. It was re-opened to trams in 1963 to take the extra Promenade and Illuminated cars, when Marton depot closed. In July 1964 a new Rigby Road entrance was made to facilitate trams to four tracks and half the depot depth, since the ambulance station was based there. In 1982, following gale-damage to the roof-supports, it was demolished from 4 November 1982, and the site became a car park. It was initially proposed that this became site for the new trams, but Starr Gate car park was chosen instead.

A final view of Blundell Street depot in 1982, with Dreadnought 59 standing on the depot approach track, in front of the Transport Office. *Author*

Pantograph 170 showing PERMANENT WAY on its indicator, in the yard of Copse Road depot on 6 July 1962, with bogies for carrying rails and other equipment. *Author*

Fleetwood - Copse Road Depot

BUILT: 1897 – with railway connection – while Tramroad being built. **CAPACITY:** 18

TRACKS: 6 **CARS:** In Company days, crossbench cars and "Box" saloons. In BCT days, Works cars and the electric locomotive operated from the depot, and used to store cars like Dreadnought 59 and Toastrack 163.

HISTORY: Constructed in 1897 for the Blackpool & Fleetwood Tramroad, and used first as a depot and then as a store. From BCT ownership in 1920, Permanent Way and coal-train was based there, and breaking-up of Toastracks and Dreadnoughts until 1939. From 1925 to 1949 coal trains were shunted to and from the rail-line and Thornton Gate siding, by electric locomotive. Permanent Way equipment was transferred to Thornton Gate in January 1963, and depot stored historic cars 2, 40, Standards 40 & 147 until closed and sold. Then it became a car salesroom site, but retains its original depot appearance.

Fleetwood – Bold Street Depot

BUILT: 1899 **CAPACITY:** 4 **TRACKS:** 2

SERVICES WORKED: In Company days, North Station & Fleetwood.

CARS: Company "Box" saloons.

HISTORY: Its construction was completed in January 1899, and the building was situated at the terminus of the Company line. Used for the last two cars to Fleetwood at night, which became the first two cars in the morning. Taken over by Blackpool Corporation in 1920, but never used as a depot. It was dewired in 1924 when the Ferry loop was constructed, and rented out. Finally it was used by "Fisherman's Friend" and demolished in 1973, flats built on the site.

Bispham Depot, Red Bank Road, Blackpool.

BUILT: 1898 **CAPACITY:** 36 **TRACKS:** 6

SERVICES WORKED: Blackpool North Station and Fleetwood service, with short workings to Cleveleys & Thornton Gate. Squires Gate & Bispham service from 1958 to 1961 in season. Starr Gate & Fleetwood service in winter months.

CARS: All Company types until 1920, Pantograph cars 167 – 176, Brush cars 284 – 303, some E.E. series 1 railcoaches. Six open Boat cars transferred from Marton Depot in March 1963. Always had overhead-line car: 4 (31), and 3 (143) from 1957 – 1963

HISTORY: Built in 1898 for Blackpool & Fleetwood Tramroad Company, and extended to double its size in 1914. Operated cars on the North Station & Fleetwood service during its history , apart from 1935 to 1940, when it was a store. An electricity generating station was attached to the depot in Company days, and a sub-station subsequently. Pantograph cars were delivered new to this depot in 1928 and Brush cars in 1940, both types being associated with this depot. In 1950 the depot was closed while the track fan was relaid and the overhead fitted above depot doors, to avoid "ducking" the trolley. During this period, Bispham cars operated from Blundell Street depot. The last service car to enter the depot on 27 October 1963 was Brush car 290, which marked the closure of the North Station route. It remained a store until 5 January 1966, when Coronation 313 was towed away by Works car 5. It was then used as an Alpic supermarket until it was demolished in 1973 for building Sainsburys supermarket. Its headstone is on display at NTM Crich, and points were taken to Heaton Park tramway for possible usage on the new depot in 2012.

A final scene at Bispham Depot in January 1966, as Coronation 313 is towed out by Works-car 5. Notice all the buildings including office, sub-station and depot.   *Author*

A view inside Marton depot in 1962 showing its clean and tidy appearance with 208 and 12. Author

Marton Depot, Whitegate Drive, Blackpool.

BUILT: 1901 **CAPACITY:** 48 **TRACKS:** 8

SERVICES WORKED: Prior to 1936 many town services operated from this depot, including Talbot Square & Layton, Talbot Square & Central Station via Marton, Talbot Square & South Pier or Royal Oak via Marton and Circular Tours. 1937 – 1962 Talbot Square & Royal Oak and South Pier in season until 1961. Circular Tours 1957 – 1961, and Promenade "specials", also "school specials".

CARS: Eight double-deck Standards, three Balloons for school-specials, Marton "Vambacs" 10-21, eight E.E. railcoaches, and twelve open "Boats".

HISTORY: Constructed in 1901 for the new Marton route to take 20 cars. Curves of the track-fan were too sharp to admit the 4-wheel Box cars, and alterations were made to the fan and the building, which increased its capacity in the same year. Initially it was an important depot for all town services, but after 1936 abandonment of Layton and Central Drive routes, it operated the Marton route and Circular Tour and supplied extra cars for the Promenade. Closed from 1939 to 1944, and used for aircraft construction by Vickers Armstrong Company. In 1951 the depot was decorated with flags for its 50th anniversary! Closed for winter from 1954 to 1959 as an economy measure. On 28 October 1962, the last service cars were 48 from Royal Oak and 40 from Talbot Square to the depot, along with illuminated 158 & 159. In 1963 depot used for scrapping trams, power switched-off on 11 March 1963 after Standard 48 left for Rigby Road. Only rear half of the depot remains, behind the petrol service station.

Rigby Road Depot, Hopton Road, Blackpool.

BUILT: 1935 **CAPACITY:** 108 **TRACKS:** 18 originally

SERVICES WORKED: Until 1961

STARR GATE & FLEETWOOD	STARR GATE & THORNTON GATE
SQUIRES GATE & CABIN	PLEASURE BEACH & BISPHAM
FLEETWOOD & CLEVELEYS	CABIN & HARROWSIDE
Until 2010: STARR GATE & FLEETWOOD	STARR GATE & CLEVELEYS

2011: PLEASURE BEACH & LITTLE BISPHAM

CARS: 27 Balloons, 25 Coronations, 10 Twin-cars, 13 OMOs, E.E. Railcoaches, Brush cars, 8 Boats – not all simultaneously! Historic cars – including Bolton 66 since 1981, B & F Box 40 1987–91 & 1998–2012. Until 2011 Stockport 5, & Sheffield 513.

HISTORY: This new depot was built under the 5-Year Plan of Modernisation, and replaced Blundell St. and Bispham depots as running-sheds. During WW 2 some of Marton cars were housed here and Bispham depot was re-opened in 1940. Tracks 15-18 were enclosed by a large partition to form an electrical compound in September 1955. Modernisation of facilities 1962-3 included a mobile washing-plant, new aluminium folding-doors to replace the roller-blind doors, extension to full-length pits, and a vacuum-cleaning plant. From 1982 track 18 was disused when an overhead-line storage was made. A body-lift is sited at the rear of track 11, to free bogies for the opposite Works fitting-shop. Today it is open-fronted and brightly-lit, and by 2012 it will only house 10 Balloons for service, Heritage trams & Illuminated trams.

A busy scene at the depot on the Open Day 28 June 1998, with a line-up of trams including Coronation 660, Pantograpgh 167, Bolton 66, Box 40 and Marton open-top 31.   *Author*

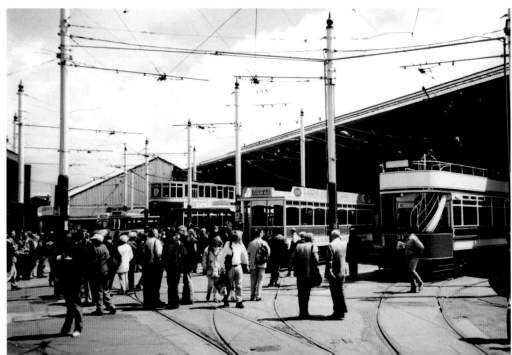

Starr Gate Depot, South Promenade.

BUILT: 2010 **CAPACITY:** 16 articulated Flexity 2 cars **TRACKS:** 7 + 3 Works

SERVICES WORKED: Starr Gate & Fleetwood or Cleveleys.

HISTORY: Work started on the depot in January 2010, after considering locations and protests by residents of the area. Planning permission was given, after the withdrawal of an additional building for 24 trams, including Balloons, Heritage & Illuminated cars. The building occupied the former car park and racing-cars site, leaving room for a loop from the terminus. The building looked striking at the end of South Promenade, with 7 tracks into the depot, offices between that and the longer Works building. When I first saw the interior in July 2011, it looked immaculate with a painted floor and pavements, and reminded me of Marton depot! The Works included 3 tracks, the centre one having gantries for overhead inspection and lift for trams. On the third track is expensive equipment for turning the wheels. On approach track round the loop is the sand-supplier and the washer, which can be set for the trams using it.

(above) Frontal view of the new depot, showing Flexity trams on each of the seven tracks. (below) A view of the new depot, with the articulated cars contrasting with Cardiff 131 on loan from the National Tramway Museum at Crich. *Author*

Tramway Museums

(above) A rare sight of 1885 conduit-car of Blackpool at Crich, operating on batteries.   *Author*

(below left) Marton open-top 31 loaded with passengers at Beamish Co. Durham in 2003.
(below right) Brush Car 623 in wartime livery seen between the trees at Heaton Park, Manchester in January 2012.   *R. P. Fergusson*

Many Are Preserved

USA
1955 - STANDARD 144 – SEASHORE TROLLEY MUSEUM.
1964 - STANDARD 48 - OREGON ELECTRIC RAILWAY.
1971 - BOAT-CAR 226 - RIO VISTA MUSEUM, CALIFORNIA.
1985 - BOAT-CAR 228 - MUNI SAN FRANCISCO – international tram service.
2000 - BOAT-CAR 660 - TROLLEYVILLE in exchange for 147, Washington Museum.
2013 - BOAT-CAR 233- MUNI SAN FRANCISCO – sold by LTT from Beamish.

UK – NATIONAL TRAMWAY MUSEUM, Crich, Derbyshire
1962 - PANTOGRAPH 167, STANDARD 49.
1963 - CONDUIT-CAR 4, B & F CROSSBENCH 2, STANDARD 40, BOX CAR 40.
1966 - ELECTRIC LOCOMOTIVE (STANDARD 158 dismantled).
1972 - TOASTRACK 166.
1977 - BRUSH-CAR 298 (restored at Salford), now stored at Clay Cross.
2000 - OMO 5 (in store at Clay Cross).
2010 - BALLOON 712 - repainted in original style - Exhibition Hall.
2011 - JUBILEE 762 - inaugurated in service 2014.
2012 - BRUSH-CAR 630 – repainted in 90s style, BOAT-CAR 236 - original style.

EAST ANGLIA TRANSPORT MUSEUM, Carlton Colville, Lowestoft.
1966 - STANDARD 159 - the first tram in service at the museum.
1969 - MARTON VAMBAC 11 - Fully-restored in 2005 & visited Beamish 2011.

OPEN-AIR MUSEUM, Beamish, Co. Durham.
1984 - MARTON OPEN-TOP 31 - restored from Works-car 4.
2011 - Balloon 703 - repainted as Sunderland 101 - bought in 2014.
2014 - BRUSH - CAR 284 - bought from Friends of Fleetwood Trams.

MANCHESTER TRAMWAY MUSEUM SOCIETY – Heaton Park.
2010 - GRINDER CAR 752, VANGUARD 619 crossbench car, formerly OMO 7.
2012 - Brush-car 623 in war-time livery), Railcoach 680 & Balloon 702.

LANCASTRIAN TRANSPORT TRUST (Transferred to Heritage Fleet)
1976 - CORONATION 327 (663) been in: Lytham, Bradford, St. Helens now depot.
2002 - ROCKET 732 - static tableau in Gynn Square until 2014, now depot.
2010 - STANDARD 143 - rebuilt as originally from works 753, now in depot.
2010 - OMO 8 - restored by LTT & BTS, and used in 2010 procession.
2010 - RAILCOACH 279 - partly restored by LTT, now in depot.

FRIENDS OF FLEETWOOD TRAMS – FUTURE MUSEUM IN FLEETWOOD
2013 - BALLOONS 710 & 726 stored on Dock Land.
2013 - TWIN - CAR 673 - 683 also stored here & Railcoach 678.
2013 - CENTENARY 641 moved to Pleasure Beach siding: displaying Bpl. Ftb Club.
2013 - CENTENARY 643 moved from Caravan Park and sold-off now.
2013 - JUBILEE 761 - moved from Fleetwood to BTS depot for future plans.
2015 - BRUSH - CARS 288 (625) & 300 (637) from Merseyside scheme storage.

Many Are Preserved continued

NORTH-EAST TRACTION TRUST (Washington Co. Durham)

2012 - BALLOONS 708 & 721 (open-top planned for 708).

2012 - TWIN-CAR 674-684   (Metro blue and yellow livery).

2012 - CENTENARY 647   (Metro livery).

2012 - HOVERTRAM 735   (Transferred from Scotland).

OTHER LOCATIONS

2015 - BRUSH-CAR 626   (Merseytravel) stored in Camell Laird Shipyard.

2014 - BRUSH-CAR 622   Norbreck School - repainted partially in Zoo livery.

2011 - CENTENARY 644   Farmer Parr's Leisure Park in Rossall.

2011 - CENTENARY 645   Windy Harbour Caravan Park.

Also - 646 Gaunt Furniture, damaged and scrapped. Balloon 716 in Perth uncertain.

LTT - BRUSH-CAR 287 (Works-Car 259) in the depot for possible future restoration.

(above) Marton Vambac 11 at East Anglia Transport Museum, with a TRAM PINCH sign and the conductor pulling the overhead-frog.   *Bryan Grint*